CISTERCIAN FATHERS SERIES: NUMBER TWO

AELRED OF RIEVAULX

Volume One

TREATISES

PASTORAL PRAYER

CISTERCIAN FATHERS SERIES

CISTERCIAN FATHERS SERIES : NUMBER TWO

THE WORKS OF
AELRED OF RIEVAULX

Volume One

Treatises

The Pastoral Prayer

introduction by

David Knowles

CISTERCIAN PUBLICATIONS

Spencer, Massachusetts

1971

Cistercian Fathers Series   ISBN 0-87907-000-5
The Works of Aelred of Rievaulx ISBN 0-87907-200-8
This volume cloth   ISBN 0-87907-202-4
         paper   ISBN 0-87907-702-6

Library of Congress Catalog Card Number: 73-152477

Copyright © Cistercian Publications, Inc., 1971

Ecclesiastical permission to publish this book has been received from Bernard Flanagan, Bishop of Worcester, December 9, 1969.

Printed in the Republic of Ireland

Cahill & Co. Limited, Parkgate Printing Works, Dublin

CONTENTS

v

EDITOR'S NOTE

IT IS WITH SPECIAL PLEASURE we present this volume not only because it is the contribution of compatriots of Aelred who carry on today on his own Island the traditions and ideals he so deeply loved and proclaims in these works, but also because it is the corporate effort of monks and nuns who find themselves on different sides of the wall that was erected on his Island in the sixteenth century. Hopefully it is one more blow that will hasten the day when that wall will completely crumble and disappear.

The translations presented here are based on the critical latin texts published by Sources Chrétiennes (see Bibliography). While English translations of *Jesus at the Age of Twelve* and *The Pastoral Prayer* have been published in recent times (again see Bibliography) the translations presented here are the first based on the critical texts. *A Rule of Life for a Recluse* was published in 1884 in a Middle English version taken from the Vernon manuscript. This was re-edited and published in part (beginning with chapter twenty-one) in 1955, but the text published here is the first complete modern English translation to be published. In these translations we have retained the divisions and paragraph numbers found in the critical editions.

We want to express our very sincere gratitude to Dom David Knowles who, though enjoying a well-earned retirement, none the less generously responded to our request to share with us his reflections on these works of Aelred. Also our debt is great to Sister

Penelope, a nun of the Congregation of Saint Mary the Virgin, who concluded a long service as a translator with her contributions in this volume and the following, volume one of the *Works of William of St Thierry*. It was this Anglican nun who first brought a number of the texts of the Cistercian Fathers into English. Our thanks go also to Sister Paul, who had to leave off her translating to respond to a call from Africa where she is now helping to implant that Cistercian contemplative life known and loved by Aelred, and to Father Theodore, of Mount Saint Bernard, who generously brought the volume to completion.

M. Basil Pennington ocso

INTRODUCTION

AILRED,[1] ABBOT OF RIEVAULX in Yorkshire, never formally canonized, but venerated in his own order and by others as a saint, was long neglected by historians and writers on the spiritual life. Now, in the last fifty years, he has become familiar to a multitude of readers in Europe and America. This interest was primarily due to the publication in 1921 by Professor F. M. Powicke of the *Life* of Ailred written by his disciple Walter Daniel. This was followed shortly by a revival of interest in the monastic history of the twelfth century, together with a rebirth of historical scholarship among the Cistercians of our day. As a consequence, most of his works have been printed and studied under many aspects. A bibliography of the manuscripts, editions and studies of Ailred has appeared, and an edition of all his works in the *Corpus Christianorum continuatio mediaevalis* is under way.

Ailred's chief attraction for the reader of today is undoubtedly his radiant and sympathetic personality, known to us both from his biographer and from the many autobiographical passages in his own writings. Our impression is confirmed by the picture, drawn by Walter Daniel and repeated in various keys by historians, of Rievaulx as the home of a group of monks who emerge from the

---

1. The conventional modern spelling of Ailred's name is Ael-, but there are several other forms in Old English and Latin. Professor Powicke followed his manuscript and wrote Ailred, which he consistently used in all his writings. Thirty years ago I followed Powicke, and to avoid inconsistency have continued to write Ailred ever since.

hooded procession of our imagination and reveal themselves as eager disputants on points of theology and philosophy, and as men moved by the personal and spiritual problems and difficulties that are common to all ages, including our own. Among them Ailred stands out as a wise and beloved father and master who himself found an answer to his problems in the monastic life before he helped to solve those of others. In addition, Ailred, thoroughly English in his loyalties and character, could write in limpid Latin that for charm of style and expression is surpassed only by St Bernard and William of St Thierry among the spiritual writers of his day. He is indeed one of the most eminent mirrors of the monastic way of life at the moment of its widest expansion and finest expression in the middle ages. Born in Northumberland *c.* 1110, he became a monk at Rievaulx in 1134 and novice master *c.* 1142. Elected founding abbot of Revesby in Lincolnshire, a daughter abbey of Rievaulx, in 1143, he returned home as abbot in 1147, and remained at Rievaulx till his death in January, 1167.

Ailred, though a born writer, did not make his début of his own choice. In 1142 he was sent to Rome by his abbot, William, once secretary of St Bernard at Clairvaux, to take part in the protest of the Cistercians against the election of Archbishop William of York, and on his way he undoubtedly called to greet the Saint at Clairvaux. A few months later Bernard wrote to him bidding him write on charity, the love of God and man, and Ailred replied with *The Mirror of Charity* (*Speculum caritatis*)[2] which many consider his greatest work (*c.* 1143). Thenceforward he continued to write: lives of saints, sermons and treatises, of which the longest was *Spiritual Friendship* (*De spirituali amicitia*),[3] in some ways a continuation of *The Mirror of Charity*. Among his other writings are the three now presented in translation.

Ailred has been called "the Bernard of the North," and he resembles his great master in several ways, in his multifarious activities, pastoral, literary, administrative, and in his sermons and letters. Like Bernard he is in many ways a contradiction of the

2. *The Works of Aelred of Rievaulx*, vol. 3 (Cistercian Fathers Series 17).
3. *The Works of Aelred of Rievaulx*, vol. 2 (Cistercian Fathers Series 5).

Cistercian program of solitude, silence and anonymity; like Bernard he remained true to his monastic observance amid both activity and infirmity. There are nevertheless many differences. Ailred, with all his gifts, was not a universal genius of the calibre of Bernard, nor was he a writer or thinker of equal power and versatility. He was not a doctor of the Church, nor the hammer of popes and delinquent bishops. His was a pure and steady candle-flame; not a blaze that could light up a dark sky or consume a forest. Yet he had a personality unique among the writers and abbots of that age. Highly gifted, strong both to do and to suffer, he was an abbot whose wisdom appeared primarily in his personal love and sympathy and his wise direction of souls. As his disciple and biographer could say: he who loved us all was deeply loved by us in return, and counted this the greatest of all his blessings.

The treatise, *Jesus at the Age of Twelve* was written *c*. 1153–7 for his friend Ivo, a monk of Wardon, a daughter house of Rievaulx in Bedfordshire. In addition to its grace and charm, it is an example of that devotion to the human life of Christ that is a feature of religious life in the twelfth and thirteenth centuries. Ailred was not wholly original; he had before him the writings of such men as John of Fécamp, St Anselm and St Bernard, but in its careful schematization for the benefit of Ivo's careful meditation, and its division into three parts—the historical explanation, the moral lessons, and the mystical interpretation—it stands in the line of the meditations which prepared the way for the affective prayer of later middle ages, which in turn, by way of Ludolf of Saxony's *Life of Christ* and Abbot Cisneros of Montserrat, led to the *Exercises* of St Ignatius. Ailred's own personal approach appears in his delineation of Jesus in his fresh boyhood. To our seeming, Ailred has in mind a boy of eight rather than of twelve—a boy whose bed is made for him by a mother who ties up his boots and pomades his hair—but it may be that a boy of twelve of Ailred's social class was very much in his mother's hands still.

The treatise, *A Rule of Life for a Recluse,* was a later work, written *c*. 1160–2. It was an answer to the repeated requests of his sister, a recluse, of whom he tells us nothing. As she had been many

years in her cell she had presumably found a regime for herself
long since, and in fact Ailred's treatise does not give a lengthy
directory. Only one of the three divisions, less than one-third of
the whole, deals with the externals of the life; the remainder consists of teaching on the virtues and a meditation on the love of God,
as called forth by the recollection of past and present benefits and
future hopes. The first part is one of the earliest English instructions
for recluses, and as such was used by many who came after, including the well known *Ancren Riwle*. In it Ailred gives a lively and
realistic description of the prevailing faults of anchoresses, from
gossiping with monks and old women, teaching children with
alternate slaps and kisses, and managing private property, to un-
seemly or downright immoral behavior, making it clear (as do
other accounts) that a recluse, who was served by a housekeeper
and an errand-maid, might take a fair share in the social life of her
neighborhood. There is no indication that the recluse's cell adjoined
the church, nor is there any mention of Mass and Communion,
which take a prominent place in the *Ancren Riwle*.

The *Meditation on Jesus* passed for long as the work of St Bernard;
the *Life of Recluses* as that of St Augustine or St Anselm, until the
edition of the Maurists. *The Pastoral Prayer,* preserved in a single
Cambridge manuscript, was attributed to its author and first
published by Dom André Wilmart as recently as 1925. It is an
outpouring of Ailred's inmost consciousness of his responsibility
for the multitude—some six hundred souls—of God's children
committed to his care, and of his inability to guide and teach each
one according to his needs. Dom Wilmart wrote of it as "one of
the most beautiful expressions of medieval devotion," and Professor
Powicke remarked that it "reveals Ailred at his best." Any abbot,
any religious superior, will find in it his own deepest apprehensions
and his own hope and trust in God.

Those who wish to know more of Ailred should consult the
recent (1969) *Aelred of Rievaulx* by Aelred Squire, OP, and the
magisterial edition of *The Life of Ailred of Rievaulx by Walter
Daniel,* by Sir Maurice Powicke, in Nelson's Medieval Classics
(Edinburgh & London, 1950; now Medieval Texts published by

Oxford University Press). For a development of the doctrine of Aelred one might well consult the work of Amédée Hallier OCSO, *The Monastic Theology of Aelred of Rievaulx* (Cistercian Studies Series 2, 1969). The three treatises in the present volume were translated into French, with excellent introductions and notes, by Dom Anselm Hoste OSB (*Quand Jésus Eut Douze Ans*, Paris, 1958), and Charles Dumont OCSO (*La Vie de Recluse* and *La Prière Pastorale*, Paris, 1961), both in the series Sources Chrétiennes. For a complete bibliography of the works, editions and manuscripts of Ailred see *Bibliotheca Aelrediana*, by Dom A. Hoste (The Hague, 1962).

David Knowles

THE COMMENTARY OF
THE VENERABLE AELRED,
ABBOT OF RIEVAULX,
ON THE PASSAGE FROM THE GOSPEL:
"WHEN JESUS WAS TWELVE YEARS OLD . . . ."

THE HISTORICAL SENSE[1]

YOU ASK ME, my dearest son Yvo,[2] to extract from the passage of the Gospel which tells what the boy Jesus did at the age of twelve some seeds of devout meditation and holy love, and, committing them to writing, as if putting them in baskets, to send them to you. While your messenger was still telling me this I became aware in the inmost depths of my heart how great and of what sort and how ardent and how sweet was the affection which inspired this fraternal request in you. Suddenly there came to mind where I had been on occasion, what I felt, what effect these same words of the gospel had on me more than once when they were read or sung. I looked back, yes, wretch that I am, I looked back and saw how far behind me I had left those sweet and pleasant experiences, how far from those delights the distractions and anxieties of business have removed me. What my soul then refused to touch is now my food in the straits in which I am.

1. For a thorough study of the senses of scripture as they would have been understood in Aelred's time, see H. DeLubac, *Exégèse Médiévale*, 4 vols., (Paris: Aubier, 1959–64).

2. Yvo, a monk of Wardon, a foundation of Rievaulx in Bedfordshire, enjoyed a special friendship with Aelred which is brought out in the first part of Aelred's book *On Spiritual Friendship*, where Yvo is one of the participants in the dialogue: "And would that your Lordship would grant me this favor, that, as often as you visit your sons here, I may be permitted, at least once to have you all to myself and to disclose to you the deep feelings of my heart without disturbance." To which Aelred replied: "Indeed, I shall do that, and gladly. For I am greatly pleased to see that you are not bent on empty and idle pursuits, but that you are always speaking of things useful and necessary

3

Remembering this I was pouring out my soul within myself,[3] when the Lord put forth his hand and touched my heart[4] and anointed it with the unction of his mercy. The very way in which you ask me will tell you what sparks of light and splendor your affection kindled in me, for you begged me to suggest to you where the boy Jesus was during those days when his mother was looking for him, where he found shelter, what food he ate, in what company he took pleasure, what business occupied him.[5] I am aware, my son, indeed I am aware with what familiarity, with what devotion, with what tears you are wont to ask these very questions of Jesus himself in your holy prayers, when you have before the eyes of your heart the sweet likeness of that dear boy, when with a certain spiritual imagination you reproduce the features of that most beautiful face; when you rejoice in the gaze of those most charming and gentle eyes bent upon you.[6] Then, I imagine, you cry out with heartfelt

---

for your progress. Speak, therefore, freely, and entrust to your friend all your cares and thoughts, that you may learn and teach something, give and receive, pour out and drink in." In view of this it is not surprising to read in no. 19 (below, p. 25) that Yvo was considered to have made great progress in the spiritual life. Yvo died before Aelred took up his pen to write the second book *On Spiritual Friendship* where we read in the opening lines: "Indeed the fond memory of my beloved Yvo, yea, his constant love and affection are, in fact, always so fresh to my mind, that, though he has gone from this life in body, yet to my spirit he seems never to have died at all. For there he is ever with me, there his pious countenance inspires me, there his charming eyes smile upon me, there his happy words have such relish for me, that either I seem to have gone to a better land with him or he seems still to be dwelling here with me on earth."—trans. M. E. Laker, Cistercian Fathers Series 5, bk. 2, n. 5.

3. Ps 41:5.   4. Job 19:21.

5. This type of devotion toward the sacred humanity of Jesus Christ was not something wholly new. It found origins in the Patristic Age in such writers as Origen and even St Jerome. However, it experienced considerable growth and development among the monastic writers of the eleventh and twelfth centuries, such as, St Anselm, Lanfranc, John of Fécamp, St Peter Damien, Ambrose of Autpert, and others. Undoubtedly it reached its climax in St Bernard and the Fathers of the Cistercian School.

6. This idea of meditating on the life of Jesus *sicut praesens* may have had its origin with St Bernard but Aelred was certainly one of the first to put it into practice. In this they were followed by such later writers as Ludolf of Saxony, pseudo-Bonaventure and St Ignatius of Loyola. See Anselm Hoste, in

devotion: "O dear boy, where were you? Where were you hiding? Who gave you shelter? Whose company did you enjoy? Was it in heaven or on earth, or in some house that you spent the time? Or did you go off with some boys of your own age into a hidden place and regale them with mysteries, in accordance with those words of yours in the Gospel: 'Allow the children to come to me and do not prevent them'?[7] If such there were, happy indeed were they to whom you accorded your company on such familiar terms for so many days."

2. But how is it, my dear Lord, that you did not have compassion on your most holy Mother as she looked for you, grieved for you, sighed for you? For she and your father looked for you in sorrow.[8] Or rather why did you, my dearest Lady, look for the boy whom you knew well was God? Were you afraid that he might be tormented by hunger, harassed by cold, or suffer some wrong from a boy of his own age? Is it not he who feeds and nourishes all things, who clothes and adorns more gloriously than Solomon the grass of the field which is there today and is cast into the fire tomorrow?[9] Indeed, my Lady, if you will allow me to say so, why did you lose your dearest Son so easily, why did you watch over him with such little care, why were you so late in noticing that he was missing? Would that Jesus himself would deign to communicate to me in what interior and spiritual words he answered you when you sought him so, on fire with such anxiety, that so I might be able to impart to you what I knew and had tasted.[10]

3. But let us consider, please, why it was that the Lord Jesus was

---

his introduction to *Aelred de Rievaulx, Quand Jésus Eut Douze Ans,* (Sources Chrétiennes, 60), pp. 7f.

7. Lk 18:16.   8. Lk 2:48.   9. Mt 6:29f.

10. *Gustata eructare.* We find the same idea coming again in Aelred's *First Sermon for the Feast of Pentecost,* ed. C. H. Talbot, *Sermones Inediti B. Aelredi Abbatis Rievallensis,* (Rome, 1952), p. 106: *Ille solus potest eructare, qui novit gustare.*—"He alone can impart who knows to taste." Aelred, perhaps draws his inspiration from Bernard of Clairvaux's *Third Sermon for Advent,* n. 2; *The Works of Bernard of Clairvaux,* vol. 4 (Cistercian Fathers Series 10).

born in Bethlehem, went into hiding in Egypt, was brought up at Nazareth and from there went up at the age of twelve to the temple and the capital. Not however alone but under parental discipline. Why was all this so? Because my Lord Jesus[11] is a leader, a doctor, a teacher. As our leader he exulted like a giant in the course he had to run, from the heights of heaven he came forth[12] and to Bethlehem he came down. Leaving traces there full of heavenly fragrance, he made darkness, that is to say Egypt, his hiding-place.[13] Then, when he had shed the light of grace from on high on men sitting in darkness and the shadow of death,[14] he ennobled Nazareth too with his holy presence. In this way made a Nazarene[15] he comes into the temple not as a teacher but as a boy who learns, who listens and asks questions, and in all this he does not withdraw himself from the control of his parents. So, Lord, so do you lead the way for wretched men, so do you heal the sick. This is the way you point out to those who are astray, this is the ladder you place for those who would mount on high, this is the return you indicate to exiles.

Who will grant me, good Jesus, to follow in your footsteps and so to run after you that eventually I may overtake you? I, yes I, am that prodigal son who took to himself his share of the inheritance,[16] for I did not wish to preserve my strength for you[17] and set out for a distant land, the region of unlikeness,[18] behaving as one of the

---

11. "My Lord Jesus"—a favorite expression of Aelred. See below n.4, p. 7; n. 23, p. 30. Aelred, perhaps, received this expression from St Augustine; see Sermon 142, 2 (PL 38:778), Sermon 88, 7 (PL 38:543).

12. Ps 18:6f. 13. Ps 17:12. 14. Lk 1:79.

15. Mt 2:23. 16. Lk 15:11ff. 17. Ps 58:10.

18. *Regio dissimilitudinis*—This is an expression which is very commonly used by the Cistercian Fathers. See William of St Thierry's *Exposition on the Song of Songs*, n. 65 and note 7 there; *The Works of William of St Thierry*, vol 2 (Cistercian Fathers Series 6), p. 52. In addition to the references given there we might also point to the *Meditations of William of St Thierry, Four*, n. 6 and *Ten*, n. 8; *The Works of William of St Thierry*, vol. 1 (Cistercian Fathers Series 3), pp. 113, 154; and his treatise, *On the Nature of Body and Soul*, *Treatises on the Soul* (Cistercian Fathers Series 24) and Isaac of Stella's *Second Sermon for the Feast of All Saints*, n. 13, *The Sermon of Isaac of Stella I* (Cistercian Fathers Series 11).

dumb beasts and made like them.[19] There I squandered all I owned in riotous living and so I began to feel want. Unhappy want, not only lacking bread but unable even to profit by the food of pigs. Following the most unclean of animals I wandered in the desert, in a waterless country, searching in vain for the way to a city I could dwell in.[20] Hungry and thirsty, my soul wasted away in suffering. Then I said: "How many hired servants in my father's house have bread in abundance, while here I perish for hunger?"[21] While I thus cried to the Lord he hearkened to me and led me into the right path, so that I might make my way to a city I could dwell in.[22] What city, but that which abounds in bread and is called the House of Bread, Bethlehem? May your mercies praise you, Lord, for you have filled the empty soul, and the hungry soul you have filled with good things.[23] You have filled it with that bread indeed which came down from heaven and was laid in the manger to become the food of spiritual animals.[24]

4. Now this is the beginning of conversion, a spiritual birth as it were, that we should model ourselves upon the Child, take upon ourselves the marks of poverty and, becoming like animals before you, Lord,[25] enjoy the delights of your presence. But because it is written: "Son, you have entered upon the service of God, take courage and prepare your spirit for temptation,"[26] the Lord Jesus

---

19. Ps 48:13. In his commentary on the account of creation in the *Mirror of Charity*, Aelred likens the evil passions in man to the wild animals which ought to be subject to him. If man rather lets them take control of him, he becomes like a beast. See the *Mirror of Charity, The Works of Aelred of Rievaulx*, vol. 3 (Cistercian Fathers Series 17), nn. 2, 26, 32.

20. Ps 106:4f.   21. Lk 15:17.

22. Ps 106:4f.   23. Ps 106:8; Lk 1:53.

24. The Eucharistic allusion which is present here is brought out more fully by Aelred in his *First Sermon for Christmas*, n. 9: "Bethlehem, the house of bread, is the holy church in which the body of Christ is administered, that is, the true bread. The manger in Bethlehem is the altar in the church. There the animals of Christ are fed . . . in this manger in the species of bread and wine is the true body and blood of Christ."

25. Ps 72:23.   26. Sir 2:1.

hides his face from us for a little while, not with the intention of leaving us, but in order to conceal himself. And now Egypt, darkness, uproar. Sitting in darkness and the shadow of death, suffering from the absence of the sweetness we used to experience, bound and shackled with iron, that is, the hardness of our own hearts, we must needs cry out to the Lord in our tribulation and he will deliver us from our straits.[27] For he scatters the darkness of this temptation with the light of his consolation and breaks the bonds of interior hardness by the grace of heartfelt compunction. With smiling face he goes before us to Nazareth, so that we may be brought up under the control of our elders amid the flowers of the Scriptures and the fruits of the virtues. There the delights which come at twelve years of age will be our lot. For just as the Lord Jesus is born and conceived in us, so he grows and is nourished in us, until we all come to perfect manhood, that maturity which is proportioned to the complete growth of Christ.[28]

5. So, "when Jesus was twelve years old, after going up to Jerusalem, as the custom was at the time of the feast, and completing the days of its observance, they set about their return home; but the boy Jesus remained in Jerusalem."[29]

In the first place, lest we fail to notice the wonderful sweetness of this most holy narrative, we must know that it was the Jews' custom that when they went up for the feast-day men and women traveled apart so that no defilement should make its way in, since God's Law prescribed that only the clean should take part in the sacred rites. We may imagine then that on that journey the boy Jesus granted the sweetness of his presence now to his father and the men with him, now to his mother and the women in whose company she was. Let us consider, I beg, how great was their

27. Ps 106:10ff.

28. Eph 4:13. Guerric of Igny speaking on this birth and growth of Jesus in us brings out a beautiful aspect, pointing out that we participate in Mary's maternity when we nurture this life within ourselves and others. See *Third Sermon for Christmas*, n. 5; *The Liturgical Sermons of Guerric of Igny I* (Cistercian Fathers Series 8), p. 52f.

29. Lk 2:42f.

happiness to whom it was given to see his face for so many days and to hear his words, sweet as honey; to contemplate in a human being, in a boy, certain signs of heavenly powers shining forth, and to intersperse their conversations with reflexions on the mystery of the wisdom which saves. The old are amazed, the young are lost in admiration, and boys of his own age are kept from mischief by the seriousness of his behavior and the weight of his words. For I think that the grace of heaven shone from that most beautiful face with such charm as to make everyone look at it, listen to him and be moved to affection. See, I beg, how he is seized upon and led away by each and every one of them. Old men kiss him, young men embrace him, boys wait upon him. And what tears do the boys shed when he is kept too long by the men? How do the holy women complain when he lingers a little longer with his father and his companions? Each of them, I think, declares in his inmost heart: "Let him kiss me with the kiss of his mouth."[30] And to the boys who long for his presence but do not dare to intrude on their elders' confabulations it is very easy to apply the words: "Who will grant me to have you as my brother, sucking my mother's breasts, to find you outside and kiss you?"[31]

6. When they all arrive in the Holy City having enjoyed this pleasure, watch, I beg, the devout and holy competition there is between one family and another as all are anxious to be granted his most lovable and charming presence. Happy the one who wins. Perhaps it was for this reason that, when the celebrations were over and they set about their return, the boy Jesus stayed on in Jerusalem without his parents' knowledge.[32] For everyone thought that he was with someone else, since he was loved by all and sought for by all, and his parents did not know that he was not there until, at the end of a day's journey, they looked for him among their kindred and friends, going from family to family of those who had gone up with them.

"Then, as they could not find him, they returned to Jerusalem

30. Song 1:1.   31. Song 8:1.

32. Lk 2:43.

and after three days they found him in the temple."[33] Where were
you, good Jesus, during those three days? Who provided you with
food and drink? Who made up a bed for you? Who took off your
shoes? Who tended your boyish limbs with oil and baths? I know,
to be sure, that as you freely willed to take our infirmity upon
yourself, so, when you so desired, you manifested your own
power; and therefore, when you so willed, you had no need of
these attentions. Where were you then, Lord? It is attractive to
form opinions or conjectures or surmises on all these matters, but
it is wrong to make any rash assertions. What shall I say, my God?
Did you, in order to conform yourself to our poverty in everything
and take upon yourself all the miseries of our human lot, beg for
alms from door to door as one of the crowd of beggars?[34] Who will
grant me a share in those crusts you obtained by begging, or at
least let me feed on the remains of that divine food?

7. But to venture on a loftier and more recondite hypothesis, on
the first day perhaps he presented himself before his Father's gaze,
not to take his seat at his side but to consult his wishes as to the
ordering of the redemptive work he had undertaken. Such a sup-
position will seem quite reasonable if the Son of God is considered
to have consulted God as man, in the likeness of a slave which he had
taken upon himself, concerning those matters which, in his divine
nature, he himself had decided together with the Father and the
Holy Spirit, coequal and consubstantial with them both as he was.
In his human littleness he would have consulted the greatness of
God not in order to learn what he knew from all eternity together
with the Father in his divine nature, but in order to defer to the
Father in everything, offer him his obedience, show his humility.
There then, in the secret dwelling-place of his Father, he disposed

33. Lk 2:44ff.

34. We find a very close parallel to this passage in Stephen of Sally's
Mirror of Novices, c. 6. Stephen in the same place explicitly acknowledges
dependance on Aelred, however, his reference is to Aelred's *Rule of Life for a
Recluse:* "What I have glossed over here, briefly and succinctly, you will find
treated in more detail in Aelred's meditations which he wrote in his short
treatise entitled, *A Rule of Life for a Recluse.*"

everything in a manner befitting God, his receiving baptism, his choosing his disciples, his inaugurating the gospel, working miracles, and finally undergoing the Passion and rising in the glory of the Resurrection. Then on the second day he granted the sweetness of his face to the choirs of angels and archangels. By informing them that the losses incurred by heaven's citizens were shortly to be made good he brought joy to the whole city of God. On the third day he visited the ranks of the Patriarchs and Prophets and confirmed, by showing them his own face, what they had already heard some time previously from the holy old man Simeon.[35] So, bringing them relief in their waiting by the promise of redemption now at hand, he made them all more patient and more cheerful.

8. It is with good reason then that at the end of the three days he was found in the temple, in the midst of the doctors and elders. As he had revealed the loving design of God the Father for men's redemption to the angels and the saints no longer in the body, as it would seem, so he began gradually to manifest the same in the most sacred of all places in the world, the temple at Jerusalem, and to those in the first place who were the guardians of this most precious treasure, the promise contained in Scripture. First listening and asking questions, then answering questions, he unfolded the most sacred mysteries. Then, we read, "all were amazed at the wisdom of his answers."[36] This is an example of humility and modesty for boys and youths, teaching them to be silent in the midst of their elders, to listen and ask questions so as to learn.

Tell me, my dearest Lady, Mother of my Lord, what were your feelings, your surprise, your joy, when you found your dearest son, the boy Jesus, not among boys but among teachers, and beheld the gaze of all eyes bent on him, everyone eagerly listening to him, while the little and the great, the learned and the ignorant alike told of his wisdom and of the answers he gave?

"I found," she says, "him whom my soul loves. I held him fast and would not let him go."[37] Hold him fast, dearest Lady, hold fast him whom you love, cast yourself upon his neck, embrace him,

35. See Lk 2:25ff.   36. Lk 2:47.   37. Song 3:4.

kiss him and make up for his absence during three days with increased delight. "Son, why have you behaved so to us? Behold, your father and I have been looking for you in sorrow."[38] Again I ask you, my Lady, why did you grieve? It was, I think, not of hunger or thirst or lack of food that you were afraid for the boy who you knew was God, it was only that you could not bear to be deprived even for a while of the ineffable delights you found in his presence. For the Lord Jesus is so dear to those who have some experience of him, so beautiful to those who look upon him, so sweet to those who embrace him, that a short absence on his part gives rise to the greatest pain.

9. "How is it," he said, "that you sought me? Did you not know that I must be concerned with my Father's business?"[39] Here already he begins to disclose the secret of the heavenly mysteries in which he had been occupied for the three days. In order to give a more clearly defined and outstanding example of humility and obedience and at the same time of readiness to give up one's own will and comply with the injunctions of elders even to one's own disadvantage, he disengaged himself from these sublime concerns, so useful and so necessary, to submit himself to the will of his parents: in the words of the Evangelist: "He went down with them and was subject to them."[40] But what is the meaning of the Evangelist's statement that "they did not understand what he had said to them"?[41] It does not, I think, apply to Mary, for from the moment the Holy Spirit came upon her and the power of the Most High overshadowed her[42] she could not be ignorant of any purpose of her Son. But while the rest did not understand what he had said, Mary, knowing and understanding, "kept all these things in her heart and pondered over them."[43] She kept them by the exercise of memory, she pondered them in her meditation, and she compared them with the other things which she had seen and heard of him. So the most blessed Virgin was even then making merciful provision for us, in order that matters so sweet, so wholesome, so

38. Lk 2:48.   39. Lk 2:49.   40. Lk 2:51.
41. Lk 2:50.   42. Lk 1:35.   43. Lk 2:51.

necessary, might not be lost to memory through any neglect and therefore not written down or proclaimed, with the result that his followers would be deprived of such delightful spiritual manna. This most prudent virgin therefore faithfully preserved all these things, modestly remained silent, then when the time came told of them and entrusted them to the holy apostles and disciples to be preached.

10. Concerning the following words: "Jesus advanced in wisdom, in years and in favor with God and men,"[44] much has been said by many persons, each according to his own judgment and it is not for me to pronounce on their opinions. Some have held that Christ's soul, from the moment it was created and taken up into God, possessed equal wisdom with God. Others, as if fearing to put a creature on a par with the Creator, have said that he advanced in wisdom just as he did in years, and they appeal to the authority of the Gospel, which says: "Jesus advanced in wisdom, years and favor."[45] And it is not surprising, they say, if he is said to have been less in wisdom, since, without any possibility of falsehood, he is stated to have been then mortal and liable to suffering and so less in beatitude. Everyone may judge of these opinions as he wills. For me it is enough to know and to believe that from the moment that the Lord Jesus was taken up into personal union with God, he was perfect God and therefore was and is perfect wisdom, perfect justice, perfect beatitude, and in addition perfect virtue. I have no doubt that whatever can be said of God as to his nature could be said of Christ, even when he was in his Mother's womb. That does not mean that we consider him before the resurrection not to have been liable to death and suffering, since we confess that he was man not merely in appearance but truly. He possessed a true human nature in which he could advance in years. But whether he could advance in wisdom is for those to decide who are competent to discuss such matters.

11. However what you are looking for, my son, is not theo-

44. Lk 2:52.   45. *Ibid.*

logical speculation but devotion; not something to sharpen your tongue but something to arouse your affections.[46] Therefore, leaving what concerns the historical sense, let us pass on to develop the spiritual sense, insofar as he of whom we are speaking will deign to inspire us.[47]

46. Aelred gives voice here to an atittude which prevails among the Cistercian Fathers. As Bernard expressed it: "My purpose is not so much to explain words as to move hearts."—*Sermon Sixteen on the Song of Songs, 1*; trans. K. Walsh, *The Works of Bernard of Clairvaux*, vol. 1, p. 114 (Cistercian Fathers Series 4). Throughout his sermons Bernard shows a willingness to allow others to decide when various opinions are legitimate.

47. The practice of tracing out first the historical sense of the scriptural passage and then passing on to the spiritual or moral teaching that can be drawn from it is common among the Cistercian Fathers and especially Bernard of Clairvaux. As Bernard expresses it himself in the opening of his *Thirty-ninth Sermon on the Song of Songs*: "In the first place it is necessary, according to my custom, to assure the sequence of the words, and the connection between the foregoing and the following. Then I shall proceed, if I can, to draw from them some consoling truths which may be useful for our moral instruction."—*The Works of Bernard of Clairvaux*, vol. 3 (Cistercian Fathers Series 7). See also the openings of Sermons 30, 42, 46, 51, 58, 59, 60, etc. We find the same approach in William of St Thierry's *Exposition on the Song of Songs*, nn. 9f., 146, *The Works of William of St Thierry*, vol. 2 (Cistercian Fathers Series 6), pp. 10, 117ff.

THE LORD OUR GOD is one God.[1] He cannot vary, he cannot change, as David says: "You are always the same and your years will not come to an end."[2] Now this God of ours, eternal, outside time, unchangeable, in our nature became changeable and entered time, in order to make the changeableness which he took upon himself for our sakes the way for changeable men, men within time, to enter into his own eternity and stability; so that in our one unique Savior there should be the way by which we might mount on high, the life to which we might come, and the truth which we might enjoy. As he himself said: "I am the way, the truth and the life."[3]

So the Lord, without ceasing to be great in his own nature, was born as a little child in the flesh and through a certain interval of time he advanced and grew up according to the flesh, in order that we who in spirit are little children, or rather almost nothing, might be born spiritually and, passing through the successive ages of the spiritual life, grow up and advance. Thus his bodily progress is our spiritual progress, and what we are told he did at each stage of his life is reproduced in us spiritually according to the various degrees of progress—as is experienced by those who advance in virtue.[4]

1. Deut 4:6.   2. Ps 101:28.   3. Jn 14:6.

4. As Aelred has already indicated above in n. 4, the mysteries of Christ are relived in us effectively. What he adds here is the fact that as one progresses in this life, one more consciously experiences this.

Let his bodily birth then be the model of our spiritual birth, that is of conversion to holiness; the persecution which he suffered at the hands of Herod, a sign of the temptation which we undergo from Satan at the beginning of our conversion; his bringing up at Nazareth, the image of our advance in virtue. In the first of these steps the Prodigal Son, wasting away with hunger, is invited to the House of Bread, and there he finds not bread made from fine wheaten flour but bread cooked in ashes, so that he may eat ashes with his bread and mix his drink with tears.[5] For bread made from fine wheaten flour is pure, clean, without ashes, without leaven, without husks—"In the beginning was the Word, and the Word was with God, and the Word was God."[6]

12. But who is capable of assimilating this? It is the bread of angels whose palate has not been dulled by tasting sour grapes. Therefore they taste and see fully and perfectly that the Lord is sweet.[7] But in order that men might eat the bread of angels, the Bread of Angels became man, taking upon himself the husks of our poverty, the ashes of our mortality, the leaven of our infirmity. He who is great became a little child, he who is rich became a poor baby; so that you who are great in your own eyes might become a little child through humility, you who are rich in your covetousness might become a poor baby. By giving up your wealth, for your spiritual rebirth you would be unable to find a place in the inn, you would not rely on your own will, your own judgment, your own knowledge, your own industry, but on the judgment of another. Then will you eat bread with ashes when the Lord feeds you with the bread of tears and gives you tears in abundance to drink.[8] So you are born in Christ and so is Christ born in you. Herod, that is the devil, is alarmed because Christ has invaded his empire. He cannot look on unmoved while his own residence is changed into a shelter for Christ. He brandishes his sword and stretches his bow, making ready in it death-dealing shafts so that he may shoot in the dark at the upright man.[9] He sets

5. Ps 101:10.   6. Jn 1:1.   7. Ps 77:25.

8. Ps 79:6.   9. Ps 7:13f.; 10:3.

the flesh on fire with nature's promptings, he harasses the mind with evil thoughts and flays with all sorts of temptations the good thoughts which in their newness are enjoying the sweet milk of first fervor. Then it will seem to you as if Christ has deserted you, until, not by your own strength but by the grace of God's compassion, Herod dies and Christ returns with increased tranquillity; he awaits your arrival in Nazareth. For after temptation you must give yourself fervently to the pursuit of the virtues and to spiritual exercises, going up as it were to Nazareth, that is to the Flower. Flower, I say, because just as the flower is not indeed the fruit but that from which the fruit is produced, so these exercises are not indeed virtues pure and simple, but from them by God's intervention true virtues are born. From there the ascent must be made to Jerusalem, but in a fitting way and at an opportune time.

13. When Jesus was twelve years old he went up to Jerusalem. It is clear, according to the laws of allegory that Christ went up from Nazareth to Jerusalem when he left the Synagogue and manifested himself in his loving kindness to the Church of the Gentiles. And it is fitting that he twelve years old then, because, coming not to abolish the Law but to fulfil it,[10] he added to the tenfold Law the two elements of evangelical perfection. He was an abbreviated Word[11] but an effective one bringing consummation to earth,[12] summing up the Law and the Prophets in the twofold commandment of charity.

14. The boy Jesus stayed on in Jerusalem, without his parents' knowledge. Christ is still in the Church, all unknown to the Jews, his parents according to the flesh. Joseph is still in Egypt and it is in the Egyptian language, not the Hebrew, that he is styled savior of

---

10. Mt 5:17.

11. Aelred has a parallel passage to this section in the first part of the *Mirror of Charity*, 1:16, n. 49, where he again speaks of the Word as *consummans et abbrevians*. The concept of the "abbreviated Word" is a constant among Cistercians. See, for example, Bernard of Clairvaux's opening lines for his *First Sermon for Christmas*, n. 1, *The Works of Bernard of Clairvaux*, vol. 4, (Cistercian Fathers Series 10).

12. Jn 19:28ff.

the world.[13] While he distributes the corn of his wisdom to the Egyptians, that is to the Gentiles, his brothers waste away with hunger for God's Word among the Canaanites, that is the unclean spirits. "They thought," we read, "that he was with the company."[14] What is this? Do you still, you Jews, presume that Christ is in your company when, according to your own Jeremiah, he has left his house and cast away his heritage, because it has become like the den of the hyena to him?[15] What signs, what mysteries, what sacraments show him still to be in your company? Where is the temple, where is the continual sacrifice, where is the priesthood, where is that altar, the only one granted to you, in Jerusalem alone? Where is that undying fire which, when it went out, involved the cessation of all holocausts at the same time, since they could not be consumed by any other fire?[16] Therefore either you have none of these or, if perhaps you claim to have them, it is not according to God's commandment that you have them and therefore you do not possess Christ either. For in all these things you did once possess Christ in the mysteries of prophecy, but when he whom they foretold appeared they were taken away and it is in vain that you lay claim to them after his coming. What amazing perversity! What amazing blindness! Paying no regard to all these things the Jews think that he is still in their company and look for him among their kindred and acquaintances. Who is it you are looking for, Jews? Who is it you are looking for?[17] Already the

13. See Gen 41:45. The Patriarch Joseph, who was rejected by his brothers, sold by them only to become the leader of a Gentile people and a savior of both Jew and Gentile alike, is considered by the Fathers as a type of Christ.

14. Lk 2:44.   15. Jer 12:7f.   16. See Lev 6:13.

17. This chiding of the Jews is not uncommon in the writings of the Cistercian Fathers, who were in this very much men of their own times. See, for example, Guerric of Igny, *Sermons Seven* and *Eight: Second* and *Third Sermons for Christmas*, Cistercian Fathers Series 8, pp. 42–53; Bernard of Clairvaux, *On the Song of Songs,* Sermons 14:8; 60:4. In this they were not anti-Semitic in the sense in which we would understand it today; indeed, Bernard staunchly defended the Jews in 1146 against the anti-Semitic persecution of Rudolph of Saxony. The approach, rather, was theological and their desire rather to increase the Gentile Christian's appreciation of that which he had so gratuitously received.

stone hewn from the mountain by no human hand has filled the
face of the earth, and are you still looking for it?[18] Behold, scattered
as you are all over the world you meet with Christ everywhere,
and are you still looking for him? Throughout all nations your
amen resounds in praise of Christ, your *alleluia* is sung, your *hosanna*
is hymned, and are you still looking for him? "He has pitched his
tent in the sun and no one can hide himself from his heat"[19] and are
you still looking for him?

You look for him among your kindred and acquaintances. You
look for him in Isaiah, but as he says: "The ox has known its
owner and the ass its master's crib, but Israel has not known me,
my people has not understood,"[20] and therefore you do not find
him. You look for him in holy David, but according to him too:
"Your table has become a snare for you"[21] and therefore you do
not find him. For your eyes have grown too dim to see and your
backs are bent.[22] You look for him in Jeremiah, but, as he bears
witness: "The priests do not know the Law nor the Seer"[23] and
therefore you do not find him. You look for him in Moses, "but
to the present day a veil is laid upon your heart when Moses is
read"[24] and therefore you do not find him.

15. So "come back, woman of Sunam, come back,"[25] come
back to Jerusalem and you will find him. Jesus is told, to be sure,
that his mother and his brethren are standing outside looking for
him:[26] does he go out to them? It is for you rather to go in and
then you will find him. "And going back," we read, "they found
him at the end of three days in the temple."[27] If the number of the
children of Israel should be like the sand on the sea-shore only a
remnant will be converted, only a remnant, I say, of Jacob, to the
strong God.[28] When? At the end of three days. O longed-for time,
when Israel shall know its God and come trembling to David its

18. Dan 2:34f. Aelred has a parallel passage to this in his *First Sermon for
the Feast of the Annunciation*, n. 2, *The Works of Aelred of Rievaulx*, vol. 4
(Cistercian Fathers Series 23).

19. Ps 18:6f.   20. Is 1:3.   21. Ps 68:23.   22. Ps 68:24.
23. Jer 2:8.   24. 2 Cor 3:15.   25. Song 6:12.   26. Mt 12:46
27. Lk 2:26.   28. Is 10:22; Rom 9:27.

C

king,[29] when both peoples shall give themselves a single head and
go up from the land.[30] When will this be, good Jesus? When will
you look upon your own flesh, those of your own blood and
your own household, for indeed no one hates his own flesh?[31]
Distribute a share, Lord, of your bread to the hungry, and bring
the needy and the wanderers into your house.[32] How long is
wretched Cain to be a wanderer and a fugitive upon your earth
which opened its mouth to drink in your blood, Abel of ours, from
his hand?[33] Have you not already payed him back seven times
over,[34] since everywhere the elder is serving the younger, everywhere the yoke weighs heavy and the sword terrifies, and there is
no one to redeem or to save? I know, yes, I know, that in the end
they will be converted and suffer hunger like dogs, but only at
evening[35] For at the end of three days they found him in the
temple.

16. The first day, on which the Lord Jesus, after entering our
Jerusalem, hid himself from his mother, the Synagogue, and his
brethren, the Jews, was the Apostles' preaching among the Gentiles,
as Paul tells the Jews themselves: "Since you judge yourselves to
be unworthy of eternal life behold we turn to the Gentiles."[36]
Then indeed light from heaven shone upon the darkened hearts of
the Gentiles, the gloomy shades of their former unbelief were
scattered and the splendor of faith shed the rays of its brightness
upon the minds of men who had been lost. But the heartening
light of this day was followed by the night of savage persecution,
when the rulers of this world raged against Christians and devised
crucifixion, fights with wild beasts, the rack, iron hooks, red-hot
gridirons, burning plates and a thousand other torments with which
to put them to death. Although the majority of Christians, strong
in their faith, laughed at all this, no small number gave way before
their torturers and were the cause of bitter grief to the saints. This
night was followed by a day bright with the light of God's compassion, when the kings of the world were converted to Christ,
the temples of the heathen were thrown down, the shrines of devils

29. Hos 395.   30. Hos 1:11.   31. Eph 5:29.   32. Is 58:7.
33. See Gen 4:12.   34. Ps 78:12.   35. Ps 58:7.   36. Acts 13:46.

were dedicated to the memory of the martyrs and, as truth gradually made its way into men's hearts, the confused night of unbelief
was dispelled. But again this brightest of days was darkened by
the clouds of perverse heresy, until the work of orthodox teachers
brought to light its errors and delivered Christian hearts from
them, so that the faith which had undergone long scrutiny and was
established by manifold reasoning could bring back to a world in
danger the Sun of Justice. And now behold it is evening and the
day draws to its close.[37] O perilous times. Already the light of the
third day is overcast by the evil life of false Christians, and as the
world grows old it is plunged into a night that overflows with
iniquity. For iniquity abounds and charity grows cold. We await the
coming of day, when through the preaching of Enoch and Elijah[38]
Jesus will be found by his mother, the Synagogue, as she enters the
temple, that is the Church, in which in the midst of the elders and
doctors there sits the Mediator of God and men, the man Christ
Jesus,[39] listening with the children, seeking with the young, teaching
with the old.

17. Then the voice of joy and exultation will resound in the
tents of Jacob,[40] when at the end of the world the true Joseph is
recognised by his brethren and the people of the Jews, like the
ageing father, are told that he is alive: "Your son Joseph is alive
and it is he who is master throughout the land of Egypt."[41]

"Son," we read, "why have you behaved so to us? Behold your
father and I were looking for you in sorrow."[42] What have you
done, Joseph? Your mother has died, your father is worn out with
continual weeping; your brethren are in danger, your father's
whole house is in sore straits. And you, regardless of your own
people, concern yourself with the welfare of the Egyptians?

"Son, why have you behaved so to us?" The brothers go into
Egypt and return, they see you as master of the land without

37. Lk 24:29.
38. There is a tradition with some basis in Scripture (See Mal 4:5ff., Sir
48:10) that Enoch and Elijah, who passed from this world without dying will
return at the end of time in order to convert the Jews to Christ.
39. 1 Tim 2:5.   40. Ps 117:15.   41. Gen 45:26.   42. Lk 2:48.

recognizing you. That beautiful face, the wonder of all Egypt, is hidden only from those of your own house and your own flesh.

"Son, why have you behaved so to us?" You look upon your own as if they were strangers, bring charges against them, threatening them with punishment, and you whom strangers find to be the mildest of men, show the utmost cruelty to your own kin.

"Son, why have you behaved so to us?" That prodigal son of yours who squandered all his property upon harlots, who committed fornication with wood and stone[43] and exchanged the glory of the imperishable God for the likeness of perishable man, of birds and quadrupeds and reptiles,[44] was welcomed to your house and for so many years now has been regaled with the meat of the fatted calf and cheered with the rich wine of the grape,[45] singing and dancing to the strains of David's music, while we, to whom belonged the covenant and the lawgiving, the worship and the promises and the fathers, we from whom you take your origin according to the flesh,[46] stand outside like strangers.

"Son, why have you behaved so to us? Behold your father and I have been looking for you in sorrow". We thought that by a fresh miracle the temple was to be rebuilt, the priesthood restored, scattered Israel summoned back to its beloved Jerusalem, and so Christ found within the borders of Judea, he whom now we find in the fields and the woods.[47]

18. "We have been looking for you in sorrow."[48] We grieved over the miracles of old, now met with no more, the oracles of the prophets now silent, the absence of any leader from the stock of Jacob,[49] the lack of anointed kings and pontiffs. Since all this proclaimed your coming, we could not believe that you would have left us and accepted the hospitality of others. Therefore "we have been looking for you in sorrow." We did not think that he who was promised to us and was given to us would have left those whom he begot to save a rival nation, would have scorned those whom he had cherished, and would have preferred peoples stained with

43. Jer 3:9.   44. Rom 1:23.   45. Deut 32:14.   46. Rom 9:4f.
47. Ps 131:6.   48. Lk 2:48.   49. See Gen 49:10.

idolatry to those who crossed the sea dryshod,[50] were fed from heaven,[51] given drink from the rock,[52] saw the waters piled up like a wall for them,[53] were able to make their way through walls,[54] found the sun obedient to them and the moon halted in its course.[55] Therefore "we were looking for you in sorrow." And at times indeed there were many signs to convince us of your coming but the call of the Gentiles and our rejection made us despair again. Therefore "we have been looking for you in sorrow."

He answers: "How is it that you were looking for me? Did you not know that I must concern myself with my Father's business?[56] O foolish and slow of heart to believe all that the prophets spoke. Was it not necessary that the Christ should so suffer and so enter upon his glory,[57] that in his name repentance should be preached through all nations?[58] Have you not heard the words of the Father to the Son as expressed by David: 'Ask of me, and I will give you the nations as your inheritance and the ends of the earth as your possession?'[59] How is it that you were looking for me and did not find me at once among the nations? Was not Abraham told: 'In your seed all the tribes of the earth shall be blessed?'[60] Did you not know that I must concern myself with my Father's business?[61]

"Listen to the Father speaking to me through Isaiah: 'It is too little for me that you should be my servant to stir up the tribes of Jacob and convert the remnant of Israel. I have made you the light of the nations, to be my salvation to the ends of the earth.'[62] Am I not for the patriarch Jacob 'the expectation of the nations'[63] and for Malachy 'he whom they desire?'[64] As the same Prophet says: 'From the rising of the sun to its setting my name is great among the nations.'[65] You were indignant at my gifts, you were jealous because I showed compassion, and the evil eye which begrudged the penitent salvation, blinded by jealousy, was unable to see the harbinger of its own salvation. Therefore I did not spare the branches native to the stock, but cut them off from the root of the

50. Ex 14:21ff.	51. Ex 16:4ff.	52. Ex 17:5ff.	53. Josh 3:14ff.
54. Josh 6:1ff.	55. Josh 10:12ff.	56. Lk 2:49.	57. Lk 24:25f.
58. Lk 24:47.	59. Ps 2:8.	60. Gen 22:18.	61. Lk 2:49.
62. Is 49:6.	63. Gen 49:10.	64. Hag 2:8.	65. Mal 1:1.

parent olive tree and grafted on other branches.[66] But now I will arise and take pity on Sion, because it is time to take pity on her, for the time has come.[67] I am calling back those whom I cast off, I am gathering together again those whom I scattered, I am welcoming those whom I rejected. 'And behold I am with you all days up to the end of the world.'"[68] Let that for the time being be enough of the allegorical sense.

66. Cf. Rom 11:17ff.   67. Ps 101:14.   68. Mt 28:20.

THE MORAL SENSE

NOW I MUST COME BACK to you, my dearest son, who have resolved to model yourself on Christ and follow closely in Jesus' footsteps. I hope to be able to explain your progress to you through this passage from the Gospel, so that you may read in these pages what you are experiencing with interior joy in yourself. For you have, I think, made the passage from the poverty of Bethlehem to the wealth of Nazareth, and, arriving at the age of twelve, you have gone up from the flowers of Nazareth to the fruits of Jerusalem. Thus you are able to study the hidden things of the spirit not so much in books as in your own experience. For as Bethlehem, where Christ was born little and poor, is the beginning of a good life, and Nazareth, where he was brought up, is the practice of the virtues, so Jerusalem, to which he went up at the age of twelve, is the contemplation of heavenly secrets.[1]

1. Aelred enters upon here what is a quite traditional yet very personal description of the three ways or three ages of spiritual growth. This tradition which goes back to Origen, and even to Saint Paul, has been developed by the different Cistercian Fathers in various ways. Indeed they do not restrict themselves to a threefold division but sometimes present fourfold divisions, or following from the Beatitudes seven steps. See, for example, Bernard of Clairvaux, *First Sermon for the Feast of All Saints*, nn. 8ff., Aelred of Rievaulx, *Third Sermon for the Feast of All Saints*; Guerric of Igny, *Sermon Fifty-three: For the Feast of All Saints*, n. 2; Isaac of Stella, *Sermons One* thru *Five: For the Feast of All Saints*, especially *Sermon Three*, nn. 10, 15. William of St Thierry discusses the three states of men of prayer at some length in his preface to the *Exposition on the Song of Songs*, nn. 13ff. (trans. C. Hart, *The Works of William of St Thierry*, vol. 2 [Cistercian Fathers Series 6], pp. 11ff., see especially note

At Bethlehem the soul becomes poor, at Nazareth it grows rich, at Jerusalem it abounds in delights. It becomes poor by perfect renunciation of the world, it grows rich by perfecting the virtues, it abounds in delights through the sweetness of what it tastes spiritually. The ascent must be made from the valley of tears, amid the difficulties of temptation, through the plains of spiritual exercise to the heights of luminous contemplation. At Bethlehem the infancy of the new way of life receives its consecration; not yet arrived at the use of reason it harms no one, deceives no one; it is free from covetousness, knows nothing of its own will, judges no one, calumniates no one, covets nothing. It is not anxious for the present nor solicitous for the future and relies only on the judgment of others. This is the infancy which the Vessel of Election[2] recommends to us in the words: "If any one among you wishes to be wise let him become foolish in order to be wise."[3] As our Lord says in the Gospel: "Unless you are converted and become like little children you shall not enter into the kingdom of heaven."[4]

20. Now if a soul has been shaped by this infancy and has passed through Herod's persecution and then begins like a fertile field to bear a rich crop of the flowers of virtue it will as a seven year old take up its proper dwelling in Nazareth, which means flower. There it will await in happiness the age of twelve.

First of all the field of our heart must be spread with manure as it were, by the remembrance of our sins and consideration of our weakness; then be worked over again and again by the plough of temptations; then the seeds of virtues will bring forth the flowers of spiritual exercises. Therefore consider the man from whom the spirit of fear has pruned away his former vices and innate covetousness as the one year old. If next the spirit of piety makes him gentle and obedient, judge him to be two years old. Then if the spirit of knowledge brings him knowledge of his own weakness

---

34): as well as in his *Golden Letter*, nn. 12ff. and *passim*. For further study of this see M. B. Pennington, "Three States of Spiritual Growth According to Saint Bernard," *Studia Monastica*, 11 (1969), pp. 315–326.

2. St Paul. See Acts 9:15.   3. 1 Cor 3:18.   4. Mt 18:3.

and a desire for God's help, have no doubt that he has reached the age of three. If the spirit of fortitude makes him unyielding and doughty against all the temptations and carnal pleasures which fight against the soul,[5] admire him as a boy of four years. Let the spirit of counsel come and by the virtue of discretion it will make him five years old. If the spirit of understanding grants him to ponder the Sacred Scripture, happy progress will bring him to the age of six. Seven years of age is brought by the spirit of wisdom, which proceeds from pondering God's Law and endows the advancing soul with four virtues as if with the light of four years. Nothing is more useful to men in their lives than these, as it is written of wisdom itself: "She teaches sobriety and prudence and justice and strength, and nothing is more useful than these."[6] For these are what govern the preceding virtues, and without them the others can neither be possessed rightly nor retained in a lasting fashion. Sobriety, for which another name is temperance, prevents any excess even in making progress in virtue. Prudence prevents one virtue being mistaken for another. Justice prevents lack of due order in the use of the virtues. Strength, for which another name is fortitude, ensures that the will remains attached to them with perseverance.

The twelfth year follows, that is the light of contemplation.[7] This raises the ardent soul to the heavenly Jerusalem itself, unlocks heaven, opens the gates of paradise, and reveals to the gaze of the pure mind the Bridegroom himself who looking out as it were through the lattice-work,[8] is more comely than the sons of men.[9]

And thus the soul deserves to hear those sweetest of words: "You are wholly beautiful, my friend, and there is no spot in you."[10] For she has been cleansed from the defilement of the passions and has

---

5. I Pet 2:11.   6. Wis 8:7.

7. It is interesting to compare the twelve stages of spiritual growth which Aelred has developed here with the seven stages considered by him and the other Cistercian Fathers in their treatment of the Beatitudes; see M. B. Pennington, "A Cistercian Way to Holiness: the Beatitudes in the All Saints Day Sermons of the Cistercian Fathers," *Cistercian Studies*, 5 (1971).

8. Song 2:9.   9. Ps 44:3.   10. Song 4:7.

escaped from the snares of business. The memory of past things has been banished. The images of outward things have disappeared and with ardent longing she raises the face of her heart in all its beauty to look upon him whom she loves. And therefore she deserves to hear: "You are wholly beautiful. . . ."

Further, "winter has passed away, the rains have abated and gone. Flowers have appeared."[11] These sweet-smelling flowers are the virtues, new as yet though they be, happily springing up in the field of the heart that is making good progress after the winter of persecutions and the rains of temptations. Delighted at once with their beauty and their fragrance Christ invites the soul to come up on high from below, in the words: "Winter has passed away, the rains have abated and gone. Flowers have appeared." And because it is through the groans of compunction that the way is opened to contemplation, he adds to what follows: "The voice of the turtle-dove has been heard in our land."[12]

21. Call to mind, my son, what you are wont to murmur in corners when, like the turtledove, which is a most chaste bird, solitary and given to lamenting,[13] you seek a retreat and, although living among many, build for yourself a daily solitude. How you moan, how you are on fire, how you seek him whom your soul loves, and, impatient in your love, long to see him whom you love. How you now cajole, now, to stimulate greater desire, are gently indignant. Now you accuse him of delay, now you complain that you are scorned, now you profess that you are unworthy of his visitation, and then again you presume on that goodness of his which you have experienced so often. Now, as if unable to hold out any longer, you try to conquer his delays by a certain spiritual wrangling or by struggling with him. What tears then, what groans, what sighs, what words. Now your eyes are heavy with tears and are raised to heaven with deep sobs; now your hands and your arms are stretched out; now you accuse your soul of sloth by

11. Song 2:11f.   12. Song 2:12.

13. Bernard of Clairvaux imputes the same characteristics to the turtle dove in his *Fortieth Sermon on the Song of Songs*, n. 4, *The Works of Bernard of Clairvaux*, vol. 3 (Cistercian Fathers Series 7).

beating your breast. Meantime words are uttered without beginning or end, incoherent, inconsistent, paying no heed to the meaning or the laws of any language. At one moment the words express your feelings, at the next moment your feelings stifle the words. Jesus to be sure, loving as he is, is glad to be overcome in such a contest. He is delighted by so great constancy in such a soul and says proudly to the angels who stand around: "The voice of the turtledove has been heard in our land."[14] For it is in the land of the living that such words of a soul on fire are heard, and the sweet fragrance of such great desire charms the whole city of God. So the same happens to you in your corner as to Elijah in his cave. First "there passed by a great and mighty wind, overturning mountains and smashing rocks," but "the Lord was not in the wind." "And after the wind an earthquake," but "the Lord was not in the earthquake." "And after the earthquake a fire," but "the Lord was not in the fire." "And after the fire the whisper of a gentle breeze."[15] These are certain steps, by which the contrite spirit ascends in prayer, like a column of smoke, all myrrh and incense and those sweet scents the perfumer knows.[16]

22. But I leave these things for you yourself not so much to investigate as to notice when you are at prayer. Remark carefully how difficult it is for you at first, sometimes, to enter into the inner room of your heart so as to find there a cave in which after a fashion you may be buried to everything which is of the world and pray to your Father in secret.[17] The heart seems on occasion to have become as hard as flint. There seems to be a mountain set before you, cutting off your inner gaze from all spiritual things, until a great and mighty wind passes by, overturns mountains and smashes rocks before the Lord. This wind is followed by an earthquake, when the spirit is softened by a certain compunction and sheds tears. Indignant with itself, it wipes away by heartfelt contrition anything in itself that it feels to be unclean. Thence there arises hope. The soul is inflamed with the fire of an unutterable longing and enters upon a certain spiritual contest with God,

14. Song 2:12.   15. 1 Kings 19:9ff.   16. Song 3:6.   17. Mt 6:6.

until the whisper of a gentle breeze makes itself felt in its inmost depths. It gently captivates the affections, imposing silence on all movements, all anxieties, all words, all thoughts; it raises the soul in contemplation up to the very gates of the heavenly Jerusalem. Then he who has been sought so long, so often implored, so ardently desired, comely of aspect beyond the sons of men,[18] looking out as it were through the lattice-work, invites to kisses: "Rise up, hasten, my friend, and come."[19] Then entering Jerusalem, the soul passes "into the place of the majestic tabernacle, as far as the house of God, with cries of exultation and thanksgiving."[20] Then there are embraces, then there are kisses, then: "I have found him whom my soul loves, I have held him fast and I will not let him go,"[21] then she abounds in delights and enjoys good things in Jerusalem, celebrating a feast day with joy and exultation.

23. I beg you therefore, my dearest son, to remember me when things are well with you, and to suggest to your Beloved, your King, who is in the holy place, that he bring me forth from this prison, from this darkness, from these chains,[22] so that at last I may be refreshed by the freedom of a purer joy. May I too feel how great is the abundance of that sweetness which he stores up for those who fear him.[23] But alas, alas, it is a moment that comes but rarely and lasts only a very short time.[24] Happy the man who can linger in these delights for three days. It is not unfitting, I think, to interpret these three days as a threefold light of contemplation, since whatever the enlightened mind can experience of God concerns, we believe, his power or his wisdom or his goodness.

And so the Lord Jesus is seen sometimes to be strong and powerful, is seen to be powerful in battle,[25] so that if you love him you may know that you will be protected by his right hand against the world, the devil and every principality and power.[26] No one can

---

18. Ps 44:3.   19. Song 2:9f.   20. Ps 41:5.

21. Song 3:4.   22. Cf. Gen 40:14.   23. Ps 30:20.

24. *Rara hora et parva mora,* a play on words which evidently Aelred borrowed from Bernard of Clairvaux. See *Sermon Twenty-three on the Song of Songs,* n. 15, *The Works of Bernard of Clairvaux,* vol. 2 (Cistercian Fathers Series 4).

25. Cf. Ps 23:8.   26. 1 Cor 15:24.

resist that right hand; they who bear the world up bow beneath it.[27] If it witholds the waters everything will be dried up, if it sends them forth they will flood the earth.[28]

24. If then a spirit endowed with power comes against you, if it inclines you to spiritual weariness,[29] if it kindles the stings of various passions, if it arouses the world against you, if it inflames persecutions, if you are afraid, if you tremble with fear, if at moments you fear being overcome, if then you run to your Jesus in your anxiety, weeping, telling him of the dangers, imploring his help, he whom you love will come to your side as a most powerful king. As David prayed: "He will take up arms and shield and arise to help you."[30] You will hear the words: "Do not be afraid of them, for I am with you."[31] But if you wish to have the knowledge of secrets or the solution of some problem revealed to you, if you wonder in bewilderment what explanation there can be for so much confusion in the world, if you are scandalized because you see sinners enjoying tranquillity, exempt from the toil of men and not scourged with their afflictions,[32] then you are seeking a retreat where you may be alone with Jesus and talk to him. You cry out with Habakkuk: "You are just, Lord, if I should dispute with you. Yet what I say to you is right. Why does the way of the godless prosper. . . ."[33] When you ask such questions the Master will come to your side. It is he alone who teaches man knowledge,[34] who opens our eyes to gaze upon the wonders of his Law.[35] It is he who has the key of wisdom, who opens so that no one can close

---

27. Job 9:13.   28. Job 12:15.

29. Aelred uses here what is a rather technical word in monastic spiritual writings: *acedia*. Monastic writers generally place this in their list of capital sins. John Cassian has perhaps most developed the consideration of this vice in his writings, devoting a full book of the *Institutes,* Book 10, to a consideration of it (*The The Institutes of John Cassian,* trans. E. Gibson, in the *Nicene and post-Nicene Fathers,* second series, vol. 11 [Grand Rapids, Michigan: Eerdmans, 1955], pp. 266ff.), as well as touching on it in the *Conferences,* e.g., Conference 5:9 (*ibid.,* pp. 342f.), 24:4 (*ibid.,* pp. 533f.).

30. Ps 34:2.   31. Jer 1:8.   32. Ps 72:3ff.

33. Jer 12:1. Aelred does seem to succumb to certain lapses of memory at times in his Scriptural attributions. For another example, see above 18, note 64.

34. Ps 93:10.   35. Ps 118:18.

and closes so that no one can open.[36] He will come in the guise of a kind doctor. In his right hand he bears the flaming Law to enlighten you with knowledge of the Law and to set you afire with that charity, which comes from meditation on the Law.

In his left hand there will be the rod of equity, the sceptre with which he reigns,[37] to charge you with presumption in your questioning and to bridle your curiosity. Finally, if all these things, great as they are and splendid and sublime, seem to be of no account since such is your longing for one kiss and one touch of his dear lips, and if you begin to complain in the Prophet's words: "I have sought your face, your face, Lord, I seek,"[38] and again: "O, that you were like a brother to me, that nursed at my mother's breasts, so that I might find you outside and kiss you!"[39] then certainly he will come to you with all the fragrance of ointments and perfumes. He will impress on your mind a certain heavenly and divine kiss. He will penetrate your inmost being with heavenly and unutterable pleasure, so that you will cry out for joy: "Graciousness is poured out on your lips."[40] When you read the Law and the Prophets, pay careful attention and you will find that these same appearances or contemplations are often portrayed there in certain figures and riddles.

25. For there are many kinds of contemplations and spiritual visions, but all of them, in my opinion, may be seen to belong either to God's power or his wisdom or his goodness. For if God be thought of as the cause of all things insofar as they exist, of certain things insofar as they are also reasonable and therefore able to be wise, of many things too insofar as they are also good, the first will be attributed to power, the second to wisdom, the third to goodness. It pertains to his power that without him no creature exists. It flows from his wisdom that without him no teaching imparts learning. It is the effect of his goodness that without him no activity is of any advantage. With him all things are secure, since there is nothing that can disturb his power. In him all things are certain, since his wisdom cannot be deceived. Everything that

36. Rev 3:7.　　　　　37. Heb 1:1.　　　　　38. Ps 26:8.
39. Song 8:1.　　　　　40. Ps 44:3.

comes forth from him is right, since no evil can corrupt his nature. Therefore in the creation of things we contemplate his power, in their form his wisdom, in their use his goodness.

Doubtless if you prefer to contemplate him in the deeds he performed in his human nature you will have no difficulty in discerning the same splendor of these three days. If with the eyes of an enlightened mind you look at him lying in the manger, crying in his mother's arms, hanging at her breasts, a little child in Simeon's arms, admire the works of his goodness. If you take pleasure in considering that countenance of fire, the whip of cords, and the awe-inspiring voice with which he terrified the buyers and sellers in the temple, overturned the seats of the money-changers and scattered their money and cast out the traders in doves,[41] stand in dread of such great power. But if you like to bring before your mind's eye the way in which the plots of the Scribes and Pharisees were so often laid bare and their crafty objections confuted by the wisdom of his answers, you will see the light of his wisdom shine forth the more brightly. So also it was by power that he put the devils to flight, fed the crowds, walked upon the sea, called Lazarus forth from the tomb, while it showed no less wisdom that in order to deceive the prince of this world he allowed himself to be tempted by the devil in the midst of miracles only a God could work, that he was hungry like one in need, that he slept in the boat, that he mounted the Cross to die.

26. However, since you linger more readily on the meditation of his goodness, enter, I beg, the house of Simon the Pharisee and watch with how loving, how gentle, how pleasant, how merciful a face he looks upon the sinful woman prostrate on the ground. With what compassion he gives her those most holy feet to wash with tears of repentance, to dry with the hair which had hitherto been the tool of pride and wantonness, gently to kiss with her lips defiled by the filth of so many sins.[42] Kiss, kiss, kiss, blessed sinner, kiss those dearest, sweetest, most beautiful of feet, by which the serpent's head is crushed,[43] before which the old enemy is cast forth,

41. Mt 21:12 and parallels.   42. Lk 7:36ff.   43. Gen 3:15.

by which vices are trodden down, before which all the glory of this world bows; those feet which tread with admirable power on the necks of the proud and the lofty. Kiss, I say, those feet, press your fortunate lips to them, so that after you no sinner may be afraid of them, no one, whatever crimes he has committed, may flee from them, no one may be overcome by the consciousness of his unworthiness. Kiss them, embrace them, hold them fast, those feet venerated by angels and men alike. Apply to them the ointment of repentance and confession, so that the whole house may be filled with the fragrance of the ointment.[44] Woe to you, Pharisee, for whom this fragrance is the smell of death, bringing death,[45] you who are afraid of being stained by the sins of another when your own pride is a much worse and more loathsome defilement. You do not realize how sweet to mercy is the wretchedness confessed to by this sinner, how welcome to loving-kindness is the sincere avowal of sin, how pleasing to it is the sacrifice of a contrite heart, what a weight of sin is consumed by burning love. For "many sins have been forgiven her because she has loved greatly."[46]

27. Thanks be to you, blessed sinner, for showing the world a safe place for its sinners, the feet of Jesus, which despise no one, reject no one, repel no one, welcome everyone, admit everyone. There indeed the Ethiopian woman takes on a fresh skin, there the leopard changes his spots:[47] it is only the Pharisee who does not spit out his pride. What are you about, my soul, my wretched soul, my sinful soul? There certainly is the place for you safely to shed your tears, to atone for your impure kisses with holy kisses, to pour out all the ointment of your devotion free from fear, without any touch or movement of vice to tempt you. Why do you hold back? Break forth, sweet tears, break forth, let no one check your flowing. Water the most sacred feet of my Savior, of my Champion. I do not care if some Pharisee mutters, if he thinks I should be kept away from his own feet, if he judges me unworthy to touch the hem of his own garment. Let him mock, let him laugh and jeer, let him turn his eyes away, let him hold his nose; for all that I will

44. Jn 12:3.   45. 2 Cor 2:16.   46. Lk 7:47.   47. Jer 13:23.

cling to your feet, my Jesus, I will hold them fast with my hands, press my lips to them, and I will not stop weeping and kissing them until I am told: "Many sins have been forgiven her, because she has loved much."[48]

28. The first day, then, on which the soul that thirsts for God dwells in the delights of contemplation as if in Jerusalem, is the consideration of God's power. The second day is admiration of his wisdom. The third day is a sweet foretaste of his goodness and kindness. To the first belongs justice; to the second, knowledge; to the third, mercy. Justice terrifies, knowledge teaches, mercy cherishes. "I will enter," says the Prophet, "into the mighty deeds of the Lord; Lord, I will remember your justice alone."[49] Behold justice. "What is uncertain and hidden in your wisdom you have manifested to me."[50] Behold knowledge. "For your mercy is better than life."[51] Behold mercy. And on the first day that fear which proceeds from the consideration of justice purifies the soul. When it has been purified wisdom enlightens it. When it has been enlightened goodness rewards it by communicating to it its sweetness. You see, if I am not mistaken, how necessary and how useful it is, amid the performance of good works, to spend these three days in the delights of Jerusalem. There fear provides you with the bread of sorrow, knowledge with the wine of exultation and goodness with the milk of consolation. I know you will not be surprised that sorrow is not absent from what I have called delights, since you have often experienced that the sorrow which proceeds from chaste fear is preferred by the contrite soul to all the delights of this world.[52] Our slight experience in the matter enables us to say as much as this. But men of more outstanding merit, endowed with greater talents and with souls better purified make more sublime and more profound discoveries in these three things. In

---

48. Lk 7:47.   49. Ps 70:16.   50. Ps 50:8.   51. Ps 62:4.

52. Bernard of Clairvaux also places a holy fear before the power and justice of God as one of the components of the experience of God in the contemplative way. See, for example, his *Twenty-third Sermon on the Song of Songs*, n. 14, *The Works of Bernard of Clairvaux,* vol. 2 (Cistercian Studies Series 4).

D

God's power they see the depths of his judgments; in his wisdom, his hidden purposes; in his goodness, the unutterable words of his mercy. So Paul, entering into the mighty deeds of the Lord and awestruck at the abyss of his judgments, says: "O man, who are you to answer God? Does the clay say to him who fashions it: 'Why have you made me so?' "[53] In wonderment too at the treasures of his wisdom he cries out: "O the depths of God's wisdom and knowledge."[54] Recalling also the wealth of his goodness, he says: "Do you scorn the wealth of his goodness and forbearance?"[55]

29. So "at the end of three days they found him in the temple."[56] That is to say, Mary and Joseph, the one his mother, the other his foster-father. He who in spirit contemplates the things of the spirit is found not just anywhere in Jerusalem but in the temple. For Jerusalem has a courtyard, it has gates, it also has a temple. While the courtyard sometimes lies open even to enemies, the gates are opened only to friends and entrance into the temple is granted only to the perfect. The man who is able to see the eternal in the things of time, the heavenly in the earthly, the divine in the human, the Creator in the creature, may exult as if admitted to Jerusalem's courtyards. This far, into the courtyard, the philosophers, like enemies, were able to penetrate with their intellectual powers as the Apostle says: "The knowledge of God is clear to their minds. For they have caught sight of his invisible nature as it is known through his creatures."[57] Whereas the man who, with veil removed[58] and his face uncovered, can look upon God's glory in Sacred Scripture, may boast that he has entered Jerusalem's gates. But if upon the altar of your heart the flame of heavenly desire has set on fire the fatness of interior love and the marrow of your affections so that fragrant smoke mounts up from your burning prayers[59] and your mind's eye extends its gaze into heaven's secret places while the palate of your heart tastes the blessed savor of God's own sweetness, then you have been in Jerusalem's temple and offered there a most acceptable holocaust.

---

53. Rom 9:20.   54. Rom 11:33.   55. Rom 2:4.
56. Lk 2:46.   57. Rom 1:19f.   58. 2 Cor 3:16.   59. Rev. 8:4.

30. But while the holy soul lingers in these delights, its mother and foster-father grieve, complain and search; when at length they find it they upbraid it with gentle reproaches and take it back to Nazareth. This can be applied in particular to those spiritual men, who have been entrusted with preaching God's Word and caring for souls. Further our foster-father I would interpret most readily as the Holy Spirit and nothing is better fitted to serve as our mother than charity. These cherish us and make us advance, feed and nourish us, and refresh us with the milk of twofold affection: love, that is, for God and for neighbor. It is these that keep and uphold us in the pursuit of holiness, as if in Nazareth, it is these that comfort us in sorrow, advise us in doubt, strengthen us when we are weary, heal the contrite of heart and bind up their wounds. It is with their help that we pass on from Nazareth to Jerusalem, from toil to rest, from the fruit of good works to the secrets of contemplation. These by the eternal law command us not wholly to neglect the contemplation of God for the sake of our neighbor's welfare, nor again to neglect our neighbor's welfare for the delights of contemplation. Therefore it is not without good reason that, if we indulge in repose more than is fitting, fraternal charity as it were complains of us. It is dissatisfied with our stay in Jerusalem if it feels that our repose is fraught with harm for others who depend on our solicitude.

For often when we lay to one side all business to give ourselves to interior meditation or to private prayer, if we linger in such delights longer than is good for those under our care, the Spirit intervenes and charity prompts us. We suddenly remember the weak and take thought for this one in distress who is waiting for fatherly consolation, that one suffering temptation and wondering when his father will appear in public and bring him some comfort by his words. Another is provoked to anger and murmuring against his father because there is no one to whom he can make the confession that will heal him, ridding him of the poison he has imbibed. And there is yet another overcome by the spirit of spiritual weariness[60] running hither and thither to find someone to talk to and

60. *Acedia*—see above n. 24, note 29, p. 31.

to advise him. It is by means of such promptings originating in our brethren's hearts, that we hear mother charity upbraiding us as it were: "Son, why have you behaved so towards us? I and your father have been looking for you in sorrow."[61] We do no wrong to the Holy Spirit or to charity when we say that they grieve or complain in holy men, even if still imperfect, since the Spirit himself intercedes for us with unutterable groanings,[62] just as he is accustomed to speak and be sorrowful and behave in holy men.

31. But if the love of repose leads the soul's feelings to murmur against such necessities, as if to say: "Ought I not to concern myself with my Father's business?" none the less the reasoning spirit considers that Christ died in order that he who lives may not live for himself. And he goes down with them in subjection to them. The man who goes down with such a foster-father and such a mother need have no fears. The man who is led by God's Spirit to put himself on the same level as his inferiors out of charity will be happy to go down. With these as my leaders I will gladly go down even to Egypt; only, if they lead me there, may they bring me back again, if they make me go down, may they make me come up again. Gladly will I submit myself to such masters, gladly will I put my shoulder to any burden they may lay upon me, gladly will I welcome the yoke they may make me bear, well aware that their yoke is sweet and their burden light.[63] But you also, my son, although Christ is still hiding you under his wings free from

---

61. Lk 2:48.   62. Rom 8:26.

63. Mt 11:30. The tension between the call to active service and the attraction to contemplation is a common theme among the Cistercian Fathers, especially those who were saddled with the burdens of the abbatial office. However Aelred's generous response here, which is typical of his great pastoral heart, is not so common. While they do not shirk their duties (although one could question William of St Thierry's resignation from office in this regard) they do more commonly lament the demands that are made upon them which take them from their cherished contemplative repose; see for example William of St Thierry, *On the Nature and Dignity of Love*, c. 8 (Cistercian Fathers Series 15); *Meditation Eleven*, n. 9, (Cistercian Fathers Series 3); *Exposition on the Song of Songs*, n. 51f. (Cistercian Fathers Series 6, see there notes 10f., p. 41.); Bernard of Clairvaux, *On the Song of Songs, Sermons Thirty, Fifty-two, Fifty-three* (Cistercian Fathers Series 7, 31).

such cares, must be as careful to avoid scandalising your companions as superiors have to be not to endanger their subjects. They on occasion put the needs of those in their care before the delights of contemplation. You must show the same preference for the unity and peace of the community. Above all never rely on your own unaided judgment to discern the times of these spiritual alterations, that is to say, when you are to go down to Nazareth or go up to Jerusalem, but always ask the advice of your elders.[64]

32. And so you have, dearest son, what you asked for. Though it is not worthy of your desire, your affection, your expectation, yet it is some token of my good will and an attempt of a sort to satisfy you. Realise that we have been concerned not so much to give an exegesis of the Gospel passage as to draw from it, as you asked, some seeds for meditation.

---

64. The importance of seeking guidance in the spiritual life has been stressed as an integral part of the monastic tradition. This has been true even from its origins in the desert, when the neophyte went there in search of a spiritual father.

HERE
BEGINS THE BOOK OF
THE VENERABLE AELRED,
ABBOT OF RIEVAULX
CONCERNING
A RULE OF LIFE FOR A RECLUSE[1]

ADDRESS

FOR MANY YEARS NOW, my sister,[2] you have
been asking me[3] for a rule to guide you in the life you have
embraced for the sake of Christ, to provide spiritual directives
and formulate the basic practices of religious life. How I wish
you had sought and obtained this from someone wiser than myself, someone whose teaching was based not on mere conjec-
ture but on personal experience. Yet by birth and in spirit I am
your brother and unable to refuse any request you make. I shall do
as you ask then, and endeavor to draw up a definite rule for you,

1. For bibliographical data on reclusion and the relation of recluses to
the Cistercian Order, see the Introduction of Charles Dumont in *La Vie de
Recluse*, Sources Chrétiennes 76 (Paris: Cerf, 1961), p. 7, note 1. For the various titles given to this treatise or letter in the manuscripts, see C. Talbot,
"The *De Institutis Inclusarum* of Aelred of Rievaulx," *Analecta S.O.C.*, 7
(1951), p. 177, note there.

2. Little is known about this sister of Aelred apart from the fact that she
was probably older than he and evidently quite dear to him. See A. Squire,
Aelred of Rievaulx: a Study (London: SPCK, 1969), pp. 118f.; Talbot, *loc.
cit.*, pp. 172f.

3. Aelred's works were more commonly written in response to a request
or an appeal from others, which seemed to insure him of an audience and
evoke his pastoral solicitude. Examples of this are the *Mirror of Charity* requested by Bernard of Clairvaux, his Father Immediate, the *Spiritual Friendship* requested by the participants in the dialogue it recounts, *Jesus at the
Age of Twelve* requested by Yvo and the *Sermons on Isaiah* which were
given at the express request of his monks.

selecting from among the various regulations of the Fathers[4] those that appear most useful in forming the exterior man. I shall add some details suited to your particular circumstances of time and place, and, wherever it seems helpful, blend the spiritual with the corporal.[5]

4. An appeal to the traditions of the Fathers is a commonplace for authors of the monastic rules. Augustine's influence, so predominant in the thinking of Aelred of Rievaulx seems to be less significant in this particular work. It is rather Jerome who has a greater impact; however his contribution passes through a mind which has been deeply influenced by Cassian, Palladius and Gregory the Great. It is the Rule of Saint Benedict, undoubtedly, which brings a certain moderation and harmony to the tendencies to exaggeration found in this tradition, something perhaps much needed for a man of Celtic background.

5. In making the distinctions between the spiritual and corporal exercises of the monastic life, Aelred would undoubtedly agree with Bernard of Clairvaux: "You may object: 'It looks as though you are so concerned with the spiritual side of things that you discredit even those material observances imposed on us by the Rule.' No, such things ought to be done, but without neglecting the others. At the same time, if it happened that one or the other element must be left aside, it is better that it be the material. For, just as the soul is more important than the body, so spiritual practices are more fruitful than material ones. But as for you, if you have become so complacent about your bodily observances that you look down on those who cannot follow suit, then it is you who are the real transgressor. You lose your grip on the more important things and cling to trifles, whereas Paul tells us to 'seek the better gifts.' . . . I don't mean by this that the external means can be over-looked, or the man who does not employ them will quickly become spiritual. Spiritual things are certainly higher, but there is little hope of attaining them or of receiving them without making use of the external exercises, . . . the man in the best position is he who makes use of both as occasion demands, and with discernment."—*Cistercians and Cluniacs: St Bernard's Apologia to Abbot William*, nn. 13f.; trans. M. Casey, *The Works of Bernard of Clairvaux*, vol. 1 (Cistercian Fathers Series 1), pp. 49ff.

PART ONE

THE OUTER MAN

YOU MUST FIRST understand the reasons that motivated
the monks of old when they instituted and adopted this form
of life. Living in a crowd means ruin for some people; for
others it will mean, if not ruin, at least injury; others again, unmoved by any apprehension, simply consider living in solitude to
be more fruitful. The monks of old then chose to live as solitaries
for several reasons: to avoid ruin, to escape injury, to enjoy greater
freedom in expressing their ardent longing for Christ's embrace.
Some lived alone[1] in the desert, supporting themselves by the work
of their hands;[2] but there were others whose confidence was
undermined by the very freedom inherent in the solitary life and
the opportunity it affords for aimless wandering. They judged it
more prudent to be completely enclosed in a cell with the entrance
walled up. So also it seemed to you when you vowed yourself to
this form of life.

But many must be either ignorant or indifferent to the true

---

1. Aelred employs here the classical phrase *soli sedebant* (cf. Lam 3:28)
which was commonly used in monastic literature to designate the eremetical
life; see, for example, in the *Apophthegmata Patrum*: Anthony, 1; Ammonias,
4; Gelasius, 6; Daniel, 8; Evagrius, 1; etc.

2. Self support was held in high esteem in the Benedictine-Cistercian
tradition inspired by the saying of the Rule of St Benedict (hereafter RB),
48:8 (for citations of RB we use the arrangement of chapter and verse of E.
Manning [Westmalle: Typis Ordinis Cisterciensis, 1962], who follows
Lentini.): ". . . then are they truly monks when they live by the labor of
their hands, as did our Fathers and the Apostles."

meaning of this life.[3] They think it enough to confine the body behind walls; while the mind roams at random, grows dissolute and distracted by cares, disquieted by impure desires.[4] The tongue too runs about all day through towns and villages, market-place and square, prying into other people's lives and behavior and into such affairs as are not only idle but often shameful.[5]

How seldom nowadays will you find a recluse alone. At her window will be seated some garrulous old gossip pouring idle tales into her ears, feeding her with scandal and gossip;[6] describing in detail the face, appearance and mannerisms of now this priest, now that monk or clerk; describing too the frivolous behavior of a young girl; the free and easy ways of a widow who thinks what she likes is right; the cunning ways of a wife who cuckolds her husband while she gratifies her passions. The recluse all the while is dissolved in laughter, loud peals of laughter, and the poison she drinks with such delight spreads throughout her body.[7] When the hour grows late and they must part both are heavily burdened, the old woman with provisions, the recluse with sensual pleasures.

Quiet returns, but the poor wretch turns over and over in her heart the fantasies born of her idle listening; her reflections only fan more fiercely the flame enkindled by her chatter.[8] Like a drunkard she staggers through the psalms, gropes through her reading, wavers while at prayer. When darkness falls she welcomes women of even less repute; they add fresh fuel to the flames and only desist when they have exposed her, now wholly ensnared by her

---

3. The use of satire was not alien to the monastic writers of the Middle Ages and abounded in the Cistercian School. Perhaps the best known examples are those found in Bernard of Clairvaux's *Apologia to Abbot William* (*op.cit.*) and his *Steps of Humility and Pride* (*The Works of Bernard of Clairvaux*, vol. 5, Cistercian Fathers Series 13). But in the passages here Aelred shows himself quite capable of keeping apace with his master.

4. Aelred addresses a similar rebuke to cenobites in his *First Sermon for the Feast of St Peter and Paul*, n. 3.

5. Cf. St Augustine, *De Opere Monachorum*, c. 28; PL 40:575f.

6. Cf. St Jerome, *Letters* 50:1; 117:10. And especially *Letter Twenty-two* to Eustochius, nn. 16, 29.

7. Cf. St Augustine, *op. cit.*, c. 22; PL 40:568f.

8. Cf. *Mirror of Charity*, II, 24 (Cistercian Fathers Series 17).

own sensuality, to the mockery of the demons. Now they speak without reserve, their purpose no longer being to arouse desire but to gratify it; together they discuss place and time, and the man who will acquiesce in her designs. The opening of the cell must somehow be enlarged to allow her to pass through or her paramour to enter; what was a cell has now become a brothel. Evidence abounds that misfortunes of this kind are only too common today among both men and women.[9]

3. Another type of recluse is the chatterbox. She may indeed shun every hint of impropriety, but she is constantly in the company of other chatterboxes. They spend the whole day indulging their curiosity, gossiping and listening to gossip—a vice which is becoming more and more prevalent today among recluses. Others, more circumspect perhaps in this regard, are yet so eager to make money or to increase the size of their flocks, are so painstaking about it and exert themselves so strenuously that they could well be mistaken for châtelaines rather than anchoresses. Finding pasture for their flocks and shepherds to tend them; demanding a statement of the numbers, weight and value of the flock's yearly produce; following the fluctuations of the market. Their money attracts money, it accumulates and gives them a thirst for wealth. The evil spirit deludes them, convinces them that it is all useful and necessary, for it enables them to give alms, to support orphans, help their families and friends and offer hospitality to their fellow-religious.

None of this is for you. You have left everything for Christ's sake. Poor with the poor, it is more fitting that you accept charity than seek elsewhere for the means of bestowing charity. It is the sign of a grave lack of faith for a recluse to be anxious about tomorrow, for our Lord says: "Seek first the kingdom of God and all these things shall be yours as well."[10]

4. A recluse must be careful to keep her mind free from anxiety and worry concerning her material needs; if it is possible she should live by the labor of her hands: this is the more perfect way.[11] But if

---

9. Cf. *Verba Seniorum, De Quiete*, II, 3; PL 73:858; St Jerome, *Letter 125* to Rusticus.

10. Mt 6:33; Lk 12:31.   11. See above note 2.

poor health or a delicate constitution forbids this[12] she should, before being enclosed in her cell, find someone to provide her with what is necessary for each day. This she may humbly accept but nothing more, even for the poor or guests—her cell is not to be besieged by beggars, nor by orphans and widows crying for alms.[13]

But who, you ask, can prevent them?

Sit still, and say nothing, wait.[14] When they realize that you have nothing, that they will get nothing from you, they will soon grow tired and depart.

"But this is inhuman!" you cry.

I tell you, if you have more food and more clothes than you need for yourself, you are no nun. So what have you to give away? The recluse is advised, then, should she earn by her own labor more than is necessary for her maintenance, to hand it over to some trustworthy person who will distribute it to the poor.[15] But I do not want anyone to approach her who might undermine her modesty, a little old woman, perhaps, mixed in with the poor, who brings her a pious token from some priest or monk, whispering flattering words in her ear and who, as she kisses her hand on receiving an alms, injects her with venom.

Moreover the recluse must guard against assuming the obligations of hospitality, even toward her sisters in religion, for along with the good there will come many of the worst type. These will install themselves at her window, and after a pious word or two by way of introduction, will settle down to talk of worldly affairs, interspersed with romance.[16] So the entire night almost will be spent without sleep. Avoid such people, take care that you are

12. Cf. RB 48:24: "Weak or sickly brethren should be assigned to tasks or crafts of such a nature as . . . not to overburden them or drive them away with excessive toil. Their weakness must be taken into consideration by the abbot."

13. Cf. Peter the Venerable, *Letter to Gilbert;* PL 189:92f.

14. *Verba Seniorum,* I, 190; PL 73:801.

15. Cf. Grimlac, *Rule for Solitaries,* c.39; PL 103:5.

16. Cf. St Jerome, *Letters* 22:24; 128:3.

never constrained to hear something you would rather not, to see things that make you shudder, for the very things that appear so unsavoury when you actually see and hear them, how sweet they seem when you reflect on them later.[17]

If you are afraid of scandalizing people because you neither give alms to the poor nor receive guests, you will find that once they learn of your resolve and how complete is your poverty, not one of them will censure you.

If indeed, despite the legitimate claims of almsgiving and hospitality, you have chosen to be poor, how much more essential it is that you limit the number of your attendants. Choose for yourself some elderly woman,[18] not someone who is quarrelsome or unsettled or given to idle gossip; a good woman with a well-established reputation for virtue. She is to keep the door of your cell, and, as she thinks right, to admit or refuse visitors; and to receive and look after whatever provisions are needed. She should have under her a strong girl capable of heavy work, to fetch wood and water, cook vegetables and, when ill-health demands it, to prepare more nourishing food. She must be kept under strict discipline, lest, by her frivolous behavior she desecrate your holy dwelling-place and so bring God's name and your own vocation into contempt.[19]

Never allow children access to your cell. It is not unknown for a recluse to take up teaching and turn her cell into a school. She sits at her window, the girls settle themselves in the porch; and so she keeps them all under observation. Swayed by their childish dispositions, she is angry one minute and smiling the next, now threatening, now flattering, kissing one child and smacking another. When she sees one of them crying after being smacked she calls her close, strokes her cheek, puts her arms round her neck and holds her tight, calling her: "My own baby girl, my own pet." There before her very eyes, even though she may not yield to them, the recluse has worldly and sensual temptations, and amid them all what

17. Cf. St Jerome, *Letter* 117:10.
18. Cf. St Jerome, *Letter* 128:3.
19. Cf. St Jerome, *Letter* 127:3; St Augustine, *De Opere Monachorem,* c·23; PL 32:576.

becomes of her continual remembrance of God?[20] For yourself, be content with the services and conversation of your two attendants.

5. Concerning the silence of recluses. I must insist on the importance of silence for a recluse. Therein lies great peace and abundant fruit. "The service of justice," Isaiah tells us, "is silence;"[21] and Jeremiah says: "It is good to wait in silence for the salvation of God;"[22] and again: "It is good for a man that he bear the yoke, let him sit alone in silence."[23] So it is written: "Listen, O Israel, and be silent."[24] You then must do as the Prophet: "I said: I will be watchful of my ways for fear that I should sin with my tongue. I will put a curb on my lips."[25] So the recluse, fearing to sin with her tongue, which, according to the Apostle James, no man can tame,[26] must put a curb on her lips; she must sit alone, imposing silence on her tongue that her spirit may speak;[27] believing that when alone she is never alone,[28] for then she is with Christ, and he would not care to be with her in a crowd.[29]

20. *Memoria Dei*—a fundamental element of the traditional monastic spirituality which finds its source in St Augustine, memory does not mean simply a calling to mind but rather a re-presentation and actual living presence of the reality somewhat as we have it in the sacrifice of the Mass in response to Christ's command: "Do this in remembrance of me." (Lk 22:19). See Aelred's *Second Sermon for the Feast of All Saints*, n. 1; *First Sermon for the Feast of the Annunciation of the Blessed Virgin Mary*, n. 1. Aelred developes his concept of the "memory of God" in many other places in his works; see Dumont, Introduction, *op. cit.*, pp. 19ff, and note 3 on p. 52.

21. Is 32:17.   22. Lam 3:26.   23. Lam 3:27f.

24. Deut 27:9 (as it is found in the Septuagint—this text is cited by St Jerome, *Letter* 125:15; PL 22:1081).

25. Ps 38:2.   26. Jas 3:8.

27. Bernard of Clairvaux in his *Forty-fifth Sermon on the Song of Songs*, n. 7, develops this idea of speaking in the spirit: "the Word is a spirit and the soul is a spirit and they have their tongues. . . ."

28. The famous expression which sums up the monastic tradition in this matter: "He will never be less alone than when he is alone," is found in the writings of St Jerome, *Adv. Iovin.*, I, 47, attributed by him to Theophrastus. It is also attributed by Cicero (*De Officiis*, III, 1) to Scipio Africanus and this came into the patristic tradition through St Ambrose (*De Officiis*, III, 2). Among the Cistercian Fathers it is taken up by William of St Thierry in his *Golden Epistle*, n. 10 (*The Works of William of St Thierry*, vol. 4, Cistercian Fathers Series 12).

29. Cf. St Augustine, *On John*, 17, 5, 11; CCL 36:176

She must sit alone then, in silence, listening to Christ and speaking with him. She must put a curb on her lips. She must take care first of all that she speak rarely,[30] then guard what she says, and finally consider to whom she speaks and in what way. She speaks only seldom, at certain fixed hours to be determined later; she must be circumspect in what she says, limiting herself to her physical needs and spiritual well-being; careful to whom she speaks, contenting herself with those specifically assigned to her for this purpose; and watchful finally of her manner, speaking humbly and with restraint, not in shrill or harsh tones, being neither smooth-tongued nor flippant.[31] If such behavior is expected of any decent man, how much more becoming is it in a woman, a virgin, a recluse.[32]

Sit in silence then, my sister, and if the needs of the body and the good of your soul compel you to speak, do so briefly, with humility and restraint.

6. Let me now indicate the people to whom you may speak. Happy the recluse who is unwilling to see or speak with a man, who has never admitted Martin.[33] But how many follow this example? A recluse today is quite satisfied if she preserves bodily chastity, if she is not drawn forth pregnant from her cell, if no infant betrays its birth by its wailing.[34]

Since it is impossible to impose a complete ban upon all converse with men, let us see to whom the recluse may justifiably speak. A priest should be provided, if this is feasible, by the neighboring monastery or church; an elderly man of mature character and good reputation. To him she may speak infrequently and solely for the purposes of confession and spiritual direction, receiv-

---

30. RB 6:3: "Therefore, since the spirit of silence is so important, permission to speak should rarely be granted even to perfect disciples. . . ."

31. Cf. RB 7:60: ". . . when a monk speaks he do so gently and without laughter, humbly and seriously, in few and sensible words, and that he be not noisy in his speech."

32. Cf. St Ambrose, *Exhortatio Virginitatis*, c. 12, 72; PL 16:357f.

33. Aelred alludes here to an incident concerning St Martin of Tours which is recounted by Sylpicius Severus in his Dialogues (II, XII); CSEL 1:194f.

34. Cf. St Jerome, *Letter* 22:13.

E

ing advice from him when in doubt and encouragement when depressed. Never must she let him touch or stroke her hand, for the evil within our very bodies is always to be feared; it can so often arouse and unman even the oldest. Never must there be any reference to thinness of face and arms or roughness of skin, lest in seeking a remedy you run a greater risk.

7. You, my sister, have never needed, thank God, to be reminded of these things. Yet I decided to include them since it was not for yourself alone that you wished me to write this rule, but also for the young girls who, on your advice, are eager to embrace a life like yours.

If someone well-known and held in high esteem—an abbot perhaps or a prior—should wish to speak to you, he should only do so in the presence of a third person. I do not want you to receive any one person too frequently nor to make such a frequent visitor the recipient of your confidences. By doing so a recluse will certainly endanger her reputation; she will endanger her peace of mind too: the more often you see the same face or hear the same voice the more indelibly does it engrave itself on your memory.[35] So the recluse should always have her face veiled when speaking with a man; she should avoid looking at him and only listen to him with fearful reserve. Listening frequently to the same man's voice can be a cause of great danger to many people.

Avoid all conversation with young men or with people of doubtful character; never permit them to speak to you unless there is real need and then only in the presence of the priest who is acting as your spiritual father. And, without his permission and express command, you should not speak to chance comers except it be a bishop, abbot or well-known prior. The very difficulties attached to speaking with you will ensure you a greater measure of peace.

Never allow messages to pass between you and any man, whatever the pretext, whether to show him kindness, to arouse his fervor, or to seek spiritual friendship and intimacy with him. Never accept letters or small gifts from a man, nor send them

35. Cf. St Jerome, *Letter* 52:5.

yourself.[36] It is a common custom now to send a young monk or priest a belt, a gaily embroidered purse, or some such thing, but this only fosters illicit affections and can cause great harm. Employ yourself rather with something necessary or servicable; the proceeds can be used for your own needs, or if you have none, given, as I have already said, to the church or the poor.

Your every word and action should be graced with modesty: it is modesty that bridles the tongue, calms an angry mood and prevents quarreling. Since a recluse should blush to speak even when it is to speak judiciously, how deeply must she blush if she allow resentment or anger to goad her into speaking injudiciously. So if people try to pick a quarrel with you, do not answer; if they speak disparagingly of you, do not retaliate; and if they provoke you, do not resist them.[37] Make light of all accusations and insinuations, whether they are made publicly or in secret; say with the Apostle in the security of a clear conscience: "It means very little to me that I should be judged by you."[38] Before all else the recluse must jealously preserve her peace of heart and tranquillity of spirit, so she shall have ever dwelling in her soul the Lord of whom it is written: "His dwelling has been established in peace."[39] Elsewhere the Lord himself says through the Prophet: "Upon whom shall my Spirit rest if not on the man who is humble and peaceful, who trembles at my words?"[40] A most holy state of soul this, but not only silly talk but also too much talk will quickly destroy it.[41] You see there is nothing you should pursue so perseveringly as silence.

8. The times for speaking and silence. I must now indicate the precise times for speaking and for observing silence.[42]

36. *Ibid.* Cf. John Cassian, *Institutes*, II, c. 16, 2f.

37. St Benedict goes a step farther: "Not to curse those who curse us, but rather to bless them."—RB 4:32.

38. 1 Cor 4:3.

39. Ps 75:3. See also Aelred's *Sermon on the Blessed Virgin Mary*, n. 2; John Cassian, *Conferences* 12:11. This reflects the early monastic tradition of *apatheia*, especially as it was brought forward by Evagrius Ponticus.

40. Is 66:2.

41. Cf. Prov 10:19.

42. Cf. Eccles 3:7. The horarium which Aelred presents here is inspired in large measure by RB, cc. 42 and 48.

From the Exaltation of the Holy Cross until Lent the recluse is to observe silence from after compline until dawn. After prime she may if she wish give her attendant directions for the day; she should do so as briefly as possible and refrain from further speech with anyone until after tierce. Between tierce and none she may speak as the occasion demands with such callers as are to be admitted, and give any further directions to her attendant. After none, when she has finished dinner, she must shun all conversation, all distraction, fearing to be condemned by those words of Scripture: "The people sat down to eat and drink, and rose up to play."[43] From vespers until collation she may again discuss any necessary matters with her attendant.

During Lent the recluse ought to maintain an unbroken silence. Since this is difficult, if not impossible, she may speak, though less often than at other times, with her confessor and attendant, but to no one else unless some important visitor arrive unexpectedly from a distance.[44]

From Easter until the Exaltation of the Holy Cross she should observe silence from compline until dawn. When the office of prime has been said she may speak with her attendant; if there are visitors with whom she should speak she may do so between none and vespers. After vespers she may again make whatever arrangements are necessary with her attendants until collation.[45]

9. Having settled that, let me now determine the hours of manual labor, reading and prayer. Idleness is indeed the enemy of the soul,[46] the enemy which more than all others the recluse must be on her guard against. It is the mother of all evils, it engenders

43. Ex 32:6.

44. A reflection of the moderation we find in RB; see 42:10, 61:1.

45. "Collation" is a monastic term for a light repast which is taken in the evening. Its origins grow out of the Rule of St Benedict where he provided that in the evening after vespers portions of the *Conferences* of Cassian (in Latin, *Collationes*) should be read while the brethren were gathering for the final office of the day, compline. The custom grew in the following centuries for the monks to take some nourishment at this time during the readings and this light meal took on the name of the readings. See RB 43:3.

46. RB 48:1.

passion, fosters the urge to roam, and nourishes vice; it nurtures spiritual weariness[47] and encourages melancholy. It is idleness that sows evil thoughts in the mind, that kindles and inflames illicit desires, that breeds distaste for quiet and disgust for the cell. Never then let the evil spirit find you idle.[48]

But as in this life we are all prey to inconstancy,[49] as we never remain long in the same state of mind,[50] we will best avoid idleness by the alternation of exercises and safeguard our peace by varying our occupations.

From November the first until Lent therefore the recluse should sleep, as near as she can judge it, until after midnight, and upon rising recite vigils as prescribed in the Rule of St Benedict[51] with as much devotion as possible. Prayer should follow and, as the Holy Spirit assists her, she will make it brief or prolonged.[52] Yet she must take care that prolonged prayer does not engender a distaste for prayer; it is more profitable to pray often and briefly than for too long at one time, unless of course it be prolonged without one's knowing it, by the inspiration of devotion.[53]

The office in honor of our Lady should follow and then the commemorations of the saints.[54] Avoid imposing on yourself the

47. *Acedia*—see above p. 31, note 29.

48. St Jerome, *Letter* 125:11.   49. Rom 8:20.

50. Job 14:2. The instability of man is brought out by Aelred in other places in his writings, e.g., *Jesus at the Age of Twelve,* n. 11, above, p. 15; *Sermon Eighteen on Isaiah (Works,* vol. 5, Cistercian Fathers Series 26).

51. RB 9.   52. RB 20:4.

53. Here in this brief paragraph on personal prayer Aelred is simply summing up the tradition as it has been expressed before him by Cassian in his *Conferences* (see especially *Conference Nine:* 25ff.). See also Gilbert of Swineshead, *Sermon Twenty-three on the Song of Songs,* n. 3, *Sermons on the Song of Songs,* Cistercian Fathers Series 14.

54. The Office of Our Lady found a place in the daily round of prayer of the Cistercians from a rather early date (see Steven of Salley, *Mirror for Novices* c. 3 and note 15 there; *Ascetical Works,* Cistercian Fathers Series 27) but only somewhat later did it become a fixed community exercise which lasted in the order until very recently. There were also commemorations of the saints which gradually grew into another office for a certain period of time but which returned to being a simple commemoration at the Office of Our Lady. See also, Conrad of Eberbach, *Cistercian Origins,* 1:27, Cistercian Fathers Series 30.

recitation of a fixed number of psalms as an obligation; when the psalms attract you use them,[55] but when they become a burden change to reading; when reading palls rouse yourself to prayer; when wearied of them all take to manual labor.[56] By this healthy alternation you will refresh your spirit and banish spiritual weariness.[57]

After the commemorations—here again the number should not be determined by vow or obligation but inspired by devotion—the recluse should spend the time that remains until dawn in manual work and the recitation of psalms. At dawn she recites lauds along with the hymns of prime. While awaiting the hour of tierce she should divide her time as devotion dictates between reading, prayer and the recitation of psalms. From tierce until none she should be employed in manual work.[58] After dinner and grace she should again alternate, as prescribed, between physical toil and spiritual exercises until vespers. Allowing a short interval after vespers, she should quietly read a little of the *Lives of the Fathers,* of their rules[59] or of their miracles; this will arouse in her a certain compunction, and so in fervor of spirit she will say compline and retire to rest with her heart filled with love.

A recluse who cannot read should devote herself all the more assiduously to manual work. After a brief period of work she must rouse herself and kneel for a few moments in prayer to God, then return at once to her interrupted task. She should do this during the time allotted both to reading and to work, often repeating the Lord's prayer and any psalms she may know while at her tasks.[60]

10. From Easter until November the first the recluse should rise

---

55. The use of the psalms in solitary and personal prayer belongs very much to the monastic tradition. See, for example, William of St Thierry, *The Golden Letter,* n. 29.

56. Cf. RB 48:23.

57. *Acedia*—see above p. 31, note 29.

58. Aelred continues to be largely inspired by the Forty-eighth Chapter of the Rule of St Benedict as he outlines this horarium for his sister.

59. The reference is undoubtedly to the *Institutes* of John Cassian. See RB 42:3.

60. Cassian, *Conferences* 9:25.

for vigils early enough to allow a very short interval between the night office and lauds.[61] The time that still remains before full daylight should be left free for prayer and psalmody. When she has recited prime she should embark upon her daily sacrifice of work until ✓ it is time for tierce. She should then occupy herself with reading until sext. After sext and dinner she can rest on her bed until none, then take up her work again until vespers; after vespers she will devote herself to prayer and the psalms, the hour for collation[62] being so arranged that she retires to bed before sunset. Whatever the time of year she must take care to go to bed before nightfall, otherwise she will be compelled to sleep on when she ought to be watching.[63]

11. Speaking now of Lent I must first, I think, emphasize its preeminence. There are many fasts observed by Christians, but the lenten fast surpasses them all, since it is imposed by divine authority not upon individuals, not upon a particular class of men, but upon all Christians.[64]

To this preeminence the Law, the Prophets and the Gospel all testify. God's servant Moses fasted forty days and forty nights that he might be worthy to receive the Law of the Lord.[65] Elijah the Prophet, when he had eaten the hearth-cake and drunk the water provided by the angel, fasted forty days and forty nights; so he was worthy to hear the voice of the Lord.[66] Our Lord and Savior too, after fasting forty days and forty nights, vanquished the tempter, while angels came and ministered to him.[67]

Fasting then is a shield no temptation can pierce; it is a ready refuge in every trial, an unfailing support for our prayers. Christ himself spoke of the great powers of fasting: when his disciples asked him why they had been unable to cast out the demon which possessed the lunatic he told them: "This kind of demon cannot be cast out except by fasting and prayer."[68]

Fasting should go hand in hand with the religious life since with-

---

61. RB 8:4.   62. See above note 45.   63. Cf. RB 41:9.
64. Cf. Aelred's *Sermon for Lent*, n. 1 (*Works*, vol. 4, Cistercian Fathers Series 23); Bernard of Clairvaux *Sermon Three for Lent*, n. 1; *Sermon Seven for Lent*, n. 4 (*Works*, vol. 8, Cistercian Fathers Series 22).
65. Ex 34:28.   66. 1 Kings 19:8ff.   67. Mt 4:2ff.   68. Mt 17:20.

out it chastity would be constantly exposed to danger. But this Lenten fast of forty days also constitutes a great sacrament: our first dwelling-place was in Paradise; our second is in this world and is filled with hardship; our third dwelling will be in heaven with the angels. Now these forty days of Lent represent the entire span of time from Adam's expulsion from Paradise until the last day, when we shall be finally liberated from this exile of ours.

Here on earth we live in fear, in toil and in grief, cast out from God's presence,[69] expelled from the joys of Paradise and forced to fast from heavenly nourishment. Ever aware of our affliction we must ever sorrow over it and show by our actions that we are but strangers and pilgrims in this world.[70] Because of our frailty we find it difficult to do this,[71] so the Holy Spirit has appointed a definite period in which we should do so, and has ordained that the Church observe certain rites that help us to realize its significance. To show us, for example, that we are exiles and are subject to death because of sin the very words God spoke to Adam when expelling him from Paradise are spoken over us as we receive the ashes: "You are dust and to dust you shall return."[72] To make us realize that while in exile we are denied the vision of God a veil is drawn between us and the Holy of Holies.[73] To remind ourselves how remote we are from the society of those whom Scripture describes: "Blessed are those who dwell in your house, O Lord, ever singing your praises,"[74] we omit our customary expression of praise: "Alleluia."[75] The stricter fast to which we are bound during this season again reminds us that in this life our desire for the heavenly bread can never be fully satisfied.

At this time then every Christian should add something to his customary service and be more diligent, more fervent in guarding

69. Ps 30:23.   70. Heb 11:13.   71. Cf. RB 49:2.   72. Gen 3: 19.

73. The practice of having a curtain between the sanctuary and the nave of the church, where the community gathered, during the Lenten season was widespread at the time Aelred wrote. In actual fact it continued to be practiced by the Cistercians until the middle of the twentieth century.

74. Ps 83:5.

75. In conformity with the Rule of St Benedict the Cistercians suppressed the usage of the *alleluia* throughout the season of Lent—RB 15.

his heart and his lips.[76] Much more so the recluse; she understands more clearly the significance of Lent insofar as her whole life is the expression of it. Desiring only during these sacred days to be pleasing to Christ and to dedicate and consecrate herself wholly to God she should deny herself every pleasure and refrain from all conversation. Let her consider this season to be her wedding day as she yearns with all her ardor for Christ's embrace. She will apply herself more frequently to prayer, throw herself more often at Jesus' feet, and by the frequent repetition of his sweet name draw forth tears of compunction and banish all distraction from her heart.

She should spend the interval between vigils and lauds in prayer and meditation.[77] When lauds and prime have been said she should devote herself to the psalms and reading until the end of the third hour, and after tierce apply herself conscientiously to manual labor until the tenth hour, interrupting her work at intervals for brief prayer. When she has said vespers and taken her meal she should recite psalms while awaiting the hour for compline.

12. As to the quality and quantity of your food and drink, it is surely unnecessary to impose any rule upon you, my sister. From your very childhood until now, when age is taking its toll of your body, you have scarcely taken enough food to keep yourself alive. I shall try however to formulate a rule for others and you can decide whether it will be helpful to them.

St Benedict allows the monk a pound of bread[78] and a hemina of wine.[79] I would not deny this to a sick or delicate recluse, but it is much better for the young and strong to abstain from any kind of wine. White bread[80] and dainty foods should also be avoided lest

---

76. Cf. RB 49:5.

77. Here again Aelred depends heavily on the Rule of St Benedict. See RB 48:14.

78. RB 39:4.

79. RB 40:2.

80. White bread was forbidden to the early Cistercians. See *Instituta Generalis Capituli*, n. 14; *Nomasticon Cisterciense,* ed. Paris-Séjelon (Solesme: St Peter's, 1892), p. 215. Cf. RB 64:19.

they poison her purity. The recluse should take counsel with necessity: satisfying her hunger without gratifying her appetite. Those who cannot achieve complete abstinence should be content with a pound of bread and a hemina of wine whether they have two meals or only one.[81]

She should have one portion of either green vegetables or beans or perhaps of porridge; the addition of a little oil, butter or milk will save it from becoming monotonous. This will be sufficient even on days when she has supper. Supper should consist of a very small portion of fish or a milk dish, or anything of this nature that is available. She should be content with a single dish, to which fresh vegetables or fruit may be added if they are obtainable;[82] these may also be eaten before the portion on days of one meal.

On vigils of feasts, on Ember Days and on the Wednesdays and Fridays out of Lent she should fast on a Lenten diet. In Lent one meal a day should suffice, and on Fridays, unless ill-health prevent her, she should fast on bread and water. From the Exaltation of the Holy Cross until Lent she should have one meal a day after none, while in Lent she should not break her fast until after vespers. From Easter to Pentecost, except for the Rogation Days and the vigil of Pentecost, she should take dinner after sext and supper in the evening; this should be the rule throughout the summer except for the Wednesdays and Fridays and solemn fasts. On these fast days in summer she may, instead of taking a midday sleep, allow herself a short rest between lauds and prime.

13. Clothing should be sufficient to ward off the cold. In winter heavier garments of skin or fur may be needed, in summer a single robe only, while throughout the year two shirts of unbleached calico or coarse linen. The veil should not be of fine or expensive material but of very ordinary black stuff: if it were colored she might appear to be making herself look attractive. She should also have such shoes, socks and clogs as she needs, yet she ought to guard her poverty so jealously that she always has just a little less than lawful necessity might allow her.

81. RB 39:4.   82. RB 39:3.

All this that concerns exterior behavior I have written my dearest sister, at your insistence. Bearing in mind not so much the fervor of the days of old as the tepidity of our own times, I have offered you a rule of life which, while tempered to the needs of the weak, allows the strong every opportunity of advancing to greater perfection.[83]

83. Cf. RB 64;19.

PART TWO

THE INNER MAN[1]

BUT NOW, WHOEVER YOU MAY be who have given up the world to choose this life of solitude, desiring to be hidden and unseen, to be dead as it were to the world[2] and buried with Christ[3] in his tomb, listen to my words and understand them.[4]

In the first place consider carefully why you should prefer solitude to the company of men. "She who is unmarried," says St Paul, "is concerned with God's claim, asking how she is to please God, intent on holiness, bodily and spiritual."[5] This is a free sacrifice, a spontaneous offering: it is not made obligatory by any law, there is no compulsion, no commandment imposes it. Therefore our Lord says in the Gospel: "Let him who can take it, take it."[6] Who is he? The man to be sure in whom the Lord has inspired this desire and to whom he grants the means of accomplishing it.

1. In the manuscripts Aelred's letter to his sister is not divided into parts. However it is clear from the final paragraph that he himself saw it clearly as made up of three sections which we, following the French translation which was published with the critical edition, have presented here as three distinct parts. See below n. 33, p. 102

2. Cf. Osbern, *The Life of St Dunstan,* 13; St Peter Damian, *The Life of St Romuald,* 64; Bernard of Clairvaux, *The Life of St Malachy* II, n. 14. Peter the Venerable, *Letters,* I, 20. In the Pontifical, even in the twelfth century, the ceremony for the walling up of a recluse was taken from the Office of the Dead.

3. Cf. Rom 6:4; Gal. 3:27; Col 2:12.

4. Cf. RB Prologue, 1; Grimlac, *Rule for Solitaries,* 2.

5. 1 Cor 7:32ff.   6. Mt 19:12.

First then, virgin, commend your good resolution with the utmost intensity to him who inspired it in you and with earnest prayer beg of him that what is impossible for you by nature may become easy through grace.[7] Bear in mind always what a precious treasure you bear in how fragile a vessel[8] and what a reward, what glory, what a crown the preservation of your virginity will bring you. In addition remember unceasingly what punishment, what shame, what condemnation the loss of it will involve.

What could be more precious than the treasure with which heaven is bought, which delights your angel, which Christ himself longs for, which entices him to love and bestow gifts? What is it he gives? I will make bold to say: himself and all that he has. Thus the spikenard of your virginity breathes out its fragrance even in heaven[9] and leads the king to desire your beauty, him who is the Lord your God.[10] See who it is you have chosen as your Bridegroom, who it is you have made your friend. He who is the most comely of the sons of men,[11] more resplendent even than the sun and than the stars in all their beauty.[12] His spirit is sweeter than honey, his inheritance surpasses the choicest honeycomb.[13] His right hand holds out length of days, his left hand wealth and glory.[14]

He it is who has already chosen you as his bride, but he will not crown you until you have been tested. Scripture says: "The man who has not been tested is not accepted."[15] Virginity is the gold, the cell is the crucible, the devil is the assayer, temptation is the fire. The virgin's flesh is the earthenware vessel in which the gold is put to be tested. If it is broken by the intensity of the heat the gold is spilt and no craftsmen can put the vessel together again.

15. With this ever in mind let the virgin guard with the utmost care and the utmost trepidation the priceless treasure of virginity which she already possesses to her advantage and which once lost cannot be recovered. Let her never cease to ponder for whose bridal chamber she is being embellished, for whose embrace she is being

---

7. Cf. RB Prologue, nn. 4, 49.   8. 2 Cor 4:7.   9. Song 1:11.
10. Ps 44:12.   11. Ps 44:3.   12. Wis 7:29.
13. Sir 24:27.   14. Prov 3:16.   15. Sir 34:9.

prepared. Let her keep before her mind's eye the Lamb she is to follow wherever he goes.[16] Let her contemplate the most blessed Mary as with the timbrel of virginity[17] she leads the dance of the virgins and entones that sweet song which none may sing but the virgins of both sexes, of whom it is written: "These are they who have kept themselves undefiled from the touch of woman, for they are virgins."[18] Do not think this means that a man cannot be defiled without a woman or a woman without a man, since that abominable sin which inflames a man with passion for a man or a woman for a woman meets with more relentless condemnation than any other crime. But virginity is often lost and chastity outraged without any commerce with another if the flesh is set on fire by a strong heat which subdues the will and takes the members by surprise.

Let the virgin always consider that all her members are consecrated to God, incorporated in Christ, dedicated to the Holy Spirit. She should be ashamed to hand over to Satan what belongs to Christ; she should blush if her virginal members are stained by even the slightest movement. Let the whole object then of her striving and of her thoughts be the preservation of her virginity, so that in her hunger for the perfection of this virtue she will consider want of food a pleasure and poverty wealth. In food and drink, in sleep, in speech let her always be on her guard against a threat to her chastity, lest by allowing the flesh more than its due she may increase the enemy's strength and nourish the hidden foe.

As she sits at table let her then meditate on the beauty of purity; in her longing for its perfection let her have no appetite for food, a veritable loathing for drink. What necessity imposes let her take with pain and shame, at times with tears. If she has to speak to someone let her always be afraid of hearing something which might

16. Rev 14:4.

17. While Aelred is here directly speaking of Mary the Mother of Christ he makes an allusion to Mary the sister of Moses, an Old Testament figure of the companion of the Savior. See Ex 15:20; also St Ambrose, *De Virginibus,* II, 2, 17; PL 16:211.

18. Rev 14:4.

cast even the least cloud over the clear skies of her chastity; let her not doubt that she will be abandoned by grace if she utters a single word against purity.

16. When you are lying on your bed commend your innocence to God and so, armed with the sign of the Cross, examine yourself on the way you have lived that day; whether you have offended the eyes of your Lord by word, deed or desire, whether you have been heedless, idle or negligent, whether you have gone beyond the limits of necessity by burdening yourself with a little too much food or indulging in drink.[19] If you find that you have been surprised by any of these things sigh over it, beat your breast,[20] and so, reconciled to your Bridegroom by this evening sacrifice, go to sleep.

If you wake up suddenly and either through the effect of sleep or by the machination of the devil you experience some bodily heat; if your wily enemy encroaches on your sleep and disturbs your conscience with evil thoughts of one sort or another; if he reminds you of pleasures and inspires you with horror of your hard life, then call to mind the blessed virgins who so often at an early age triumphed over their godless foe. Think of St Agnes,[21] who reckoned gold, silver, expensive clothes, precious stones and all the pomp of worldly glory as so much dung.[22] When she was summoned to the judgment-seat she did not hold back. She despised the judge's blandishments and laughed at his threats, afraid rather of being spared than of being punished. Happy she who turned a brothel into an oratory, while the angel who entered together with the virgin flooded the darkness with light and punished with death the man who sought to corrupt her. If then you also pray and take up the arms of your tears against him who incites you to impurity, you may be sure that the angel who was present in the brothel will not be absent from your chaste cell. It is hardly sur-

19. Cf. St Augustine, *On Nature and Grace,* 38:45; PL 44:269.

20. In a time when frequent confession of venial sins was not a yet common practice such sacramental forms as striking one's breast was still fully appreciated as a means of obtaining remission of venial sins.

21. Cf. St Ambrose *De Virginibus,* 1, 2, 5ff.; PL 16:189ff.; Cistercian Breviary, Feast of St Agnes (January 21), Second Nocturn.

22. Cf. Phil 3:8.

prising that this material fire of ours could not burn St Agnes; the flame of the flesh had died in her, she was consumed by the fire of charity.

Whenever you are troubled by warmth of passion, whenever the evil spirit suggests anything unlawful, remember that he who searches hearts and reins[23] is present and his eyes gaze upon whatever you are doing or thinking. Show reverence then for the angel who, without any doubt, stands at your side and answer the tempter: "I have God's angel as my beloved and he watches over my body with jealous care."[24]

When you are in distress such as this, let more severe fasting reinforce your efforts, for when the flesh is sorely afflicted there can be little or no pleasure.

17. Let no one deceive himself, let no one flatter himself, let no one have any illusions: the young never obtain or keep chastity without great contrition of heart and bodily affliction. Even in the sick and the aged it is not safe from danger. It is true that continence is a gift of God and no one can be continent unless God grant it to him. This is a gift which is not to be attributed to any merit of our own but to his free grace. Yet he judges as unworthy of so great a gift those who refuse to undergo any toil to obtain it, expecting to remain chaste in the midst of pleasures, continent as they feast, free from temptation while consorting freely with young women. They would load themselves with unclean humors in banqueting and drunkenness[25] without being defiled, attach fire to themselves and escape burning.[26] A difficult thing, or would you say even impossible?

18. I know a monk[27] who at the beginning of his monastic life was afraid of threats to his chastity from the promptings of nature,

23. Ps 7:10.

24. Cistercian Breviary, Feast of St Cecilia (November 22), Antiphon for Prime.

25. Rom 13:13.

26. Prov 6:27. Cf. St Jerome, *Letter* 22:14; *Letter* 52; St Gregory the Great, *Dialogues*, 3:7.

27. Aelred would here seem to be speaking about himself; Cf. *Sermon Twenty-three on Isaiah; Mirror of Charity*, I, 28.

from the force of bad habit and from the suggestions of the wily
tempter, and so declared war on himself, was filled with savage
hatred for his own flesh and sought nothing more than what would
afflict it. Accordingly he weakened his body by fasting, and by
depriving it of its lawful due suppressed its simplest movements.
But when he was forced by weakness to allow himself more, the
flesh came to life again and upset the tranquillity which he thought
he had acquired. Often he plunged into cold water and stayed there
for some time singing psalms and praying.[28] Frequently too when
he felt forbidden movements he rubbed his body with nettles and
so, by inflaming his bare flesh, overcame the inflammation of lust.[29]

When all this proved of no avail and the spirit of fornication still
harassed him he applied the one remaining remedy and, prostrate
at Jesus' feet, he prayed, wept, sighed, implored, besought, insisted
that he either kill him or heal him. He cried out repeatedly: "I will
not go away, I will not be quiet, I will not let go of you until you
bless me."[30] He was granted some temporary relief but refused
lasting tranquillity. For while the irregular movements of the flesh
died down for a little, his heart was beset with forbidden affections.
My God, what crosses, what tortures that wretched man then
endured, until in the end he came to find such joy in chastity that
he conquered all the pleasures of the flesh that can be experienced
or imagined. But then also it was only for a time that he was
delivered, and now when sickness is added to old age he still
cannot flatter himself that he is safe.

19. How shameful then is the effrontery of some who, grown
old in uncleanness, will not even forego the company of undesir-
able persons. Dreadful as it is to say, they share the same bed with
them, embrace them and kiss them, and yet declare they have no
fear for their chastity because their body has grown cold and their

28. Ascetical immersions were used quite frequently by monks in England
during the eleventh, twelfth, and thirteenth centuries. See L. Gougaud,
Dévotions et Pratiques Ascétiques du Moyen âge (Maredsous, 1925), p. 162f.

29. For a parallel in the life of St Benedict see St Gregory the Great,
Dialogues, 2:2; PL 66:132.

30. Gen 32:26.

F

members are powerless to commit sin.[31] Unhappy are they and more wretched than all mortal men who, although they are no longer capable of carrying out the evil deed, have their wills still attached to its uncleanness.[32] The passage of time brings with it no slackening in their desires although they are powerless to carry them into effect. Yet is what they say true, or is wickedness bearing false witness, showing up two sins in its efforts to conceal one? For men in extreme old age sometimes suffer nocturnal imaginings, and the stirrings of the flesh often make themselves felt even in those to whom years have brought diminished powers.

20. As for you, sister, I would have you never rest secure but always be afraid. Beware of your weakness and like the timid dove go often to streams of water where as in a mirror you may see the reflection of the hawk as he hovers overhead and be on your guard.[33] The streams of water are the teaching of Scripture, flowing from the clear fountain of wisdom. It makes you aware of the devil's promptings and teaches you how to take due precautions. For nothing is better for preventing useless ideas or driving out impure imaginations than the study of God's Word. The virgin should make herself so familiar with it that she is incapable of occupying her mind with anything else even when she wishes to do so.[34] Let her be thinking over the Scriptures when she falls asleep, let something from the Scriptures be the first thought to come to mind when she wakes up; as she sleeps let her dreams be interspersed with some verse from the Scriptures which has remained fixed in her memory.[35]

21. Now there are some who are impeded in the practice of virtue by a certain fear that overmuch fasting or undue lack of

31. Cf. St Jerome, *Letter* 22:14; St Augustine, *Regula Monachorum*.
32. Cf. St Jerome, *Letter* 22:7.
33. Cf. St Ambrose, *De Virginibus* II, 27.
34. Cf. St Jerome, *Letters* 22:17; 125:11.
35. William of St Thierry gives similar advice to the Carthusians of Mont Dieu; *The Golden Letter*, nn. 31, 34 (*Words*, vol. 4, Cistercian Fathers Series 12). They are following here the whole of the monastic tradition, see, for example, John Cassian, *Conference*, 1:17; *Institutes*, 2:14f.; St Jerome, *Letter* 22:37; Cesarius of Arles, *Rules for Recluses*, 22.

sleep may deprive them of vigor and so make them a burden to others as well as a sorrow to themselves. This is the way we invent excuses for our sins.[36] How few there are today, indeed how few, who are set on fire by such fervor. We are all wise, all prudent, all discreet. We sniff war from afar and are in such dread of bodily disease before it makes itself felt that we take no notice of the spiritual sickness which is already troubling us—as if the flame of lust were easier to bear than the complaints of the stomach; as if it were not much better to avoid the wantonness of the flesh by continual weakness than to be brought into subjection to it in health and strength. What difference does it make whether it be by fasting or by sickness that the pride of the flesh be tamed and chastity preserved? "But we must be on our guard against relaxation," it will be said, "lest perhaps on the grounds of infirmity we may be led astray by the attractions of pleasure." But you may be sure that the man who feels weak, who is ill, whose bowels are wrung, whose stomach is dried up, will find any pleasure more of a burden than a delight.[37]

22. I have known a man who in his youth through force of habit was unable to contain himself. Then at length taking stock of himself he became mightily ashamed. Forthwith his heart grew hot within him and as he pondered fire broke out.[38] Wholesome anger with himself led him to a fierce attack upon himself; he declared war upon his body and deprived it even of what seemed to be necessary. Flippancy gave way to seriousness, talkativeness to silence. After that no one saw him making jokes, no one beheld him laughing, no one heard an idle utterance come forth from his mouth. He felt such contempt and loathing for temporal consolations and anything he thought might be pleasing to the flesh that he did not allow himself any rest or any comfort from food and

---

36. Ps 140:4.   37. Cf. above, n. 16, p. 66.

38. Ps 38:4. Aelred here might well be speaking of a friend of whom he spoke in the *Spiritual Friendship*, bk. 2, nn. 119ff. Both Powicke (Walter Daniel, *The Life of Ailred of Rievaulx*, [London 1950] Introduction, p. lxvii) and J. Dubois (Aelred of Rievaulx, *L'Amitié Spirituelle* [Brouges, 1948] Introduction p. lxxxviii) identify this friend as Geoffrey of Dinant.

drink. So anxious and so scrupulous was he over his thoughts that he seemed to go to excess, though only in this respect. Standing, sitting and walking he so kept his face cast down and his eyes bent on the ground that he seemed to be standing in fear and trembling before God's judgment seat. With arms such as these he won a glorious triumph over the tyrant. For, having developed very serious stomach trouble, after a long illness as the hour of his death approached he said: "Let it be: behold, Jesus is coming."

23. I do not say this in disparagement of discretion, the mother and nurse of all the virtues.[39] But we must keep within due limits those things which provide material for vice: eating, sleeping, bodily relaxation, familiarity with women and effeminate men, and sharing their company; we often use discretion as a pretext to disguise the pursuit of pleasure. True discretion is to put the soul before the body and where both are threatened and the health of the one can only be obtained at the price of suffering for the other, to neglect the body for the sake of the soul.[40]

My purpose in making these observations has been to make you aware of the care you must take to preserve your chastity. Yet, although it is the flower and adornment of all the virtues, it withers and fades away without humility.

24. This is the sure and safe foundation of all the virtues, and whatever is not built upon it will fall in ruins. The beginning of all

---

39. Cassian, *Conferences* 2:4.

40. See a parallel passage to this in the *Mirror of Charity,* 3:37. For an example of this in Aelred's own life see Walter Daniel, n. 41; ed. Powicke, p. 50. This is common teaching among the Cistercian Fathers. See for example William of St Thierry, *Exposition on the Song of Songs,* n. 128; *The Golden Letter,* n. 18; Guerric of Igny, *The Liturgical Sermons,* 1:6; 3:4; 5:6; 11:2. Bernard of Clairvaux in his *Book on Precept and Dispensation* brings out an important distinction: "Again we read, 'the corruptible body weighs down the soul.' Note well that it is said of the 'corruptible' body rather than simply of the body, since it is the corruption which constitutes the burden."—n. 59; *Monastic Obligations and Abbatial Authority: St Bernard's Book on Precept and Dispensation, Works,* vol. 1, Cistercian Fathers Series 1, p. 148. To place Aelred's thought in its full context see the article of C. Dumont, "L'équilibre humain de la vie cistercienne d'après le Bx. Aelred de Rievaulx" in *Collectanea O.C.R.,* 18 (1965), pp. 188f.

sin is pride,[41] which drove the angels out of heaven and man out of Paradise. From this evil root there spring many branches, but they are all divided into two kinds, carnal and spiritual. Carnal pride is to pride oneself on the things of the flesh, spiritual pride is to pride oneself on the things of the spirit.

Carnal pride furthermore is subdivided into two kinds, boasting and vanity.[42] It is a question of vanity if Christ's handmaid prides herself in her thoughts on the fact that she was born of noble parents,[43] if she takes pleasure in the fact that she has preferred poverty to riches for Christ's sake, if she tries to put herself before those who are poorer and less well-born than she is, if she considers that she has achieved something great in despising a wealthy marriage. Another kind of vanity consists in the pleasure given by a certain show of decoration inside the cell: walls adorned with paintings or gilt work, the oratory embellished with a variety of hangings and statues. Beware of all these things as contrary to your profession.[44]

How can you dare to take pride in riches or noble birth when you seek to appear as the bride of him who became poor although he was rich[45] and chose for himself a poor mother, a poor family, a poor little house also and the squalor of the manger? Is it any matter for pride that you have preferred the Son of God to the sons of men, that you have despised the uncleanness of the flesh for the beauty of virginity, that you have exchanged things which will become mere dung for the eternal riches and delights of heaven?

If you must glory, glory in the Lord[46] and serve him in fear.[47] But I would not have you pursue, on the pretext of devotion, the glory which expresses itself in paintings or carvings, in hangings decorated with birds or animals or flowers of one sort and another. Leave such

41. Sir 10:15.

42. For a description of boasting see Aelred's *Fourth Sermon for the Feast of St Benedict*, n. 6.

43. St Jerome, *Letter* 22:27.

44. The concern which Aelred shows here for interiority pertains very much to the whole of his spiritual outlook and to monastic tradition in general, especially that of the Cistercians. Cf. *Mirror of Charity*, 2:24.

45. 2 Cor 8:9.   46. 1 Cor 1:31.   47. Ps 2:11.

things to people who have nothing within themselves in which to glory and so must seek their pleasure in outward things.

25. For all the glory of the king's daughter is within, clad as she is in robes decked with borders of woven gold.[48] If you are already the King's daughter, since you are the bride of the King's Son, and have heard the Father's voice saying: "Listen, daughter, and see and incline your ear,"[49] let all your glory be from within. See that your glory be the witness of your conscience.[50] There let there be the fair array of the virtues, let it be there that colors of one sort and another so blend in harmony that one may increase the beauty of another and that which of its own nature is less brilliant may shine more brightly in comparison with another. Let chastity be combined with humility and nothing could be more splendid. Let simplicity be added to prudence and nothing could be more dazzling. Let mercy be joined with justice and nothing could be more pleasing. Ally modesty with courage and nothing could be more useful. Keep the eyes of your mind occupied with this array of virtues, make it your whole concern to nurture it in your soul. Then if you attach borders of woven gold to it you will have made yourself a many-colored robe[51] in which your Bridegroom will delight to see you. The border is the part at the edge, the end as it were of a garment.[52] But the end of the Law is charity, coming from a pure heart and a good conscience and unfeigned faith.[53]

26. Let it be in these that you glory and find your happiness; within, not without, in true virtues, not in paintings and statues.

Your altar should be covered with white linen cloths. Their whiteness will betoken chastity and display simplicity. Consider what toil, what poundings it took to rid the linen of the earthy color in which it grew up and to bring it to such whiteness that it could adorn an altar, cover Christ's body. We are all born with the color of earth since: "I was conceived in iniquity and in my sins

---

48. Ps 44:14f.   49. Ps 44:11.
50. 2 Cor 1:12. These same texts were used by Bernard of Clairvaux in his *Sermon Twenty-five on the Song of Songs*, n. 7 to present the same doctrine.
51. Gen 37:3.   52. St Isidore, *Entomology*, 24, 20.
53. 1 Tim 1:5.

did my mother conceive me."[54] In the first place linen is steeped in water, and in the waters of baptism we are buried together with Christ.[55] There sin is destroyed but infirmity remains unhealed. We are given some whiteness by the forgiveness of our sins, but because of our natural corruption, which remains, we are not yet fully rid of our earthy color. When it is taken out of the water linen is dried, for after the waters of baptism the body has to be macerated by fasting and so emptied of unlawful humors. Next linen is pounded with hammers, and our flesh is wearied by many temptations. After this linen is threshed with iron nails so that it may shed its superfluous covering, and when we have been scraped with the teeth of regular observance we are scarcely left with the necessaries. Then linen passes through a gentler process of refining by means of softer teeth, and we, having overcome the worst passions with great toil, are cleansed from lighter and everyday sins by simple confession and satisfaction. Then linen is drawn out in lengths by spinners and we are drawn on to what lies ahead by patience and perseverance. Further, in order that its beauty may be perfect, fire and water are applied to it, and we have to pass through the fire of tribulations and the water of compunction in order to arrive at the refreshing coolness of chastity.[56]

Let these be the thoughts which the furnishings of your oratory suggest to you, instead of feasting your eyes on unbecoming fantasies. On your altar let it be enough for you to have a representation of our Savior hanging on the Cross; that will bring before your mind his Passion for you to imitate, his outspread arms will invite you to embrace him, his naked breasts will feed you with the milk of sweetness to console you.

If you like, in order to bring home to you the excellence of virginity, a picture of the Virgin Mother and one of the Virgin Disciple may stand on either side of the Cross, so that you may consider how pleasing to Christ is the virginity of both sexes, con-

---

54. Ps 50:7.   55. Rom 6:3f.

56. It is evident that Aelred was familiar with the process of preparing linen; perhaps this would indicate that it was one of the industries of Rievaulx.

secrated in his Mother and the Disciple he loved[57] more than the others. Therefore as he hung on the cross he brought them together in so close a union as to give her to the Disciple as a mother and him to his Mother as a son.[58] O how blessed is John in this legacy: with all the solemnity of a last will and testament he is given the fair flower of the whole human race, the hope of the world, the glory of heaven, the refuge of the wretched, the comfort of the afflicted, the consolation of the poor, the salvation of the despairing, the reconciliation of sinners, in a word the mistress of the world and the queen of heaven.

Let these things serve to increase your charity, not to provide empty show. From all of them you must ascend to unity, for only one thing is necessary.[59] That is the one thing, the unity which is found only in the One, by the One, with the One with whom there is no variation, no shadow of change.[60] The man who unites himself with him becomes one spirit with him,[61] passing into that unity which is always the same and whose years do not come to an end.[62] This union is charity, as it were the edge and border of the spiritual vesture.

27. Indeed the nuptial robe, woven out of all the array of the virtues, ought to have borders of gold, that is, of charity in all its brilliance. It should contain all the virtues and bring them together into unity. It should impart to one and all its own splendor and make the many into one, uniting with the many to the One, so that all may no longer be many but one.

Now charity has two divisions, love of God and love of one's neighbor.[63] Further, love of one's neighbor has two subdivisions, innocence[64] and beneficence, that is, to do no harm to anyone and to do good to those to whom you are able.[65] It is written: "What you would not have done to yourself do not to another"[66]—and

57. Jn 19:26.   58. Jn 19:27.   59. Lk 10:42.

60. Jas 1:17. See parallel expressions of Aelred's aspiration and esteem for unity in the *Mirror of Charity*, 3:1.

61. 1 Cor 6:17.   62. Ps 101:28.   63. Lk 10:27.

64. See *Mirror of Charity*, 3:5.   65. Tob 4:6.

66. Mt 7:12; Lk 6:31; RB 4:9; 70:7.

this is innocence. Our Lord says in the Gospel: "Everything that you
would have men do to you, do you also to them"[67]—and this is
beneficence.

Take good heed how these two things concern you. First you are
to harm no one, then you are not to desire to harm anyone. The
first is easy for you, since it is something not in your power to do,
unless perhaps you inflict injury with your tongue. The second will
not be difficult if you keep your way of life and love the poverty
which you have vowed. For there cannot be any ground for ill will
towards anyone when there is no covetousness, when nothing is
loved that might be taken away,[68] nothing taken away that ought
to be loved.

Then wish well to everyone, be of service to those to whom you
can. And how is that possible, you will say, since I am not allowed
to possess the least thing which I might give to those in need?[69]

28. Recognize the state in which you are, dearly beloved. There
were two sisters, Martha and Mary. The one was busy, the other
was at leisure. The one gave, the other asked. The one was anxious
to serve, the other nourished her affections. She did not walk about
or run hither and thither, was not concerned with the reception of
guests, not distracted by household worries, not busy with answering cries of the poor. She just sat at Jesus' feet and listened to what
he had to say.[70] This is your portion, dearly beloved. Dead and
buried to the world, you should be deaf to all that belongs to the
world and unable to speak of it. You should not be distracted but

---

67. Mt 7:12.

68. Cf. *Mirror of Charity*, 1:31.

69. Isaac of Stella asks the same question though with greater development
and eloquence in his *Third Sermon for the Feast of All Saints*, n. 13.

70. Lk 10:38ff. The contrast of Martha and Mary, the former representing
the active life and concern and the latter a type of the contemplative life, is
a constant throughout the monastic tradition. See for example St Augustine,
Tract on John, 124:5; St Gregory, *Homily on Ezechiel*, II, II, 9. It is found
throughout the writings of the Cistercian Fathers, e.g., Bernard of Clairvaux,
Cistercians and Cluniacs; St Bernard's Apologia to Abbot William, nn. 5 (see
there especially n. 24), 13; William of St Thierry, *Meditation* 11:9; Guerric
of Igny, *Sermon Fifty: Fourth Sermon for the Feast of the Assumption*, nn. 3f;
Isaac of Stella, *Second Sermon for the Feast of All Saints*, nn. 17ff.

absorbed, not emptied out but filled up. Let Martha carry out her part; although it is admitted to be good, Mary's is declared better. Did Mary envy Martha? Rather it was the other way about. So let those who seem to make the best out of living in the world envy your life; it is not for you to envy theirs.

The giving of alms belongs to those who have earthly possessions or who have been entrusted with the administration of Church property. For what was given to Holy Church by the faithful is handed over to bishops, priests and clerics to be distributed, not hidden away or appropriated, but given in alms. Whatever they have belongs to the poor, to widows and orphans, and to those who minister at the altar and so have the right to live from the altar. The gifts too which are made to monasteries for the use of Christ's servants should be administered by persons appointed for the purpose, so that what remains over when the needs of the brethren have been satisfied is not stored up in coffers but given away to guests, pilgrims and the poor. This is the concern of those who are entrusted with Martha's functions, not of those who with Mary are left free to enjoy a leisure that will be profitable to their souls. So monks of the cloister[71] should not be troubled with any concern for the poor or distracted by the reception of guests; indeed they should not even have any care for the morrow,[72] no anxiety over food and drink. Let them rather feed on saffron[73] and take their pleasure in the things of the spirit. It is for those who are thought little of and therefore appointed as judges[74] to betake themselves to the dungheap.[75] They are the oxen with whose dung the slothful man is pelted.[76] For there are some who grow weary of spiritual things like the Jews in the desert and feel a loathing for the manna

71. Aelred uses here a rather technical word: *claustrales.* These were the simple monks who had nothing other to do than to live the integrally contemplative life within the enclosure of the monastery. They were distinguished from the *oboedientiales,* the monks who had the responsibility of taking care of the temporalities and also the spiritual charges of the monastery, and the *praelati* or the superiors of the monastic community. See Aelred's *First Sermon for the Feast of St Peter and Paul,* n. 2.

72. Mt 6:34.   73. Lam 4:5.   74. I Cor 6:4.
75. Lam 4:5.   76. Sir 22:2.

from heaven.[77] When they see others busy about temporal affairs they envy them, criticize them, complain of them and, on account of the dung which soils them, are pricked by bitter jealousy. If it should chance that any such should be charged with the administration of temporal affairs it is to them that the words can fittingly be applied: "They who were fed with saffron have betaken themselves to the dungheap."[78]

If then even those who live in community and have not a little in common with Martha are not allowed to be busy about many things, how much less will it be allowed to you who have withdrawn from the world to the fullest extent and are forbidden not only to possess but even to see or hear what belongs to the world? For since no one gives you anything to distribute in alms, from what source will you come to possess anything you might give away? If your work yields something, give it away not by your own hand but by that of some other person. If your food comes from others what right have you to give away what belongs to them, since you are not allowed to take anything more than what you need for yourself?

What good then will you be able to do to your neighbor?[79] Nothing is more valuable, a certain holy man has said, than good will.[80] Let this be your offering. What is more useful than prayer? Let this be your largesse. What is more humane than pity? Let this be your alms. So embrace the whole world with the arms of your love and in that act at once consider and congratulate the good, contemplate and mourn over the wicked. In that act look upon the afflicted and the oppressed and feel compassion for them. In that act call to mind the wretchedness of the poor, the groans of orphans, the abandonment of widows, the gloom of the sorrowful, the needs of travellers, the prayers of virgins, the perils of those at sea, the

77. Num 20:5. 78. Lam 4:5.

79. The answer which Aelred gives to this question is one of the most beautiful passages in this letter to his sister. For another very beautiful response to this same question see Isaac of Stella, *Third Sermon for the Feast of All Saints,* nn. 13ff.

80. St Gregory the Great, *Fifth Homily on the Gospel,* n. 3; PL 76:1094.

temptations of monks, the responsibilities of prelates, the labors of those waging war. In your love take them all to your heart, weep over them, offer your prayers for them. Such alms are more pleasing to God, more acceptable to Christ, more becoming your profession, more fruitful to those who receive them. The performance of such good works as these help you to live out your profession instead of upsetting you; they increase the love you have for your neighbor instead of diminishing it; they are a safeguard, not an obstacle to tranquillity of mind.

What more can I say when holy men, in order to love their neighbors perfectly, made it their concern to have nothing in this world, to desire nothing, and not even to possess things without attachment. You will recognize the words: they come from St Gregory.[81] See how many think the opposite. For in order to carry out the law of charity they seek to have something to give away, whereas St Gregory awards the perfection of charity to those who resolved to have nothing, to desire nothing, not to possess anything even without being attached to it.

---

81. *Ibid., n. 4.*

PART THREE

THE THREEFOLD MEDITATION

AFTER THESE CONSIDERATIONS on the love of our neighbor I will add a few words on the love of God. Although both of the sisters loved God and their neighbor, Martha concerned herself especially with the service of her neighbors, while Mary drank from the fountain of divine love.[1] There are two elements in the love of God, interior dispositions and the performance of works. The latter consists in the practice of the virtues, the former in the sweetness tasted by the spirit. The practice of the virtues is a matter of a rule of life, fasts, vigils, work, reading, prayer, poverty and such like, while the affections are nourished by wholesome meditation.[2] So, if that sweet love of Jesus is to grow in your affections, you need a threefold meditation, on the past, the present and the future, that is to say, you must call to mind what happened long ago, experience the present and look forward to what lies in the future.[3]

1. Cf. St Gregory, *On Morals in Job*, Book 7, c. 37; PL 75:764; Homilies on Ezechiel, III, 9; PL 76:809.

2. This is the distinction between the active and contemplative life as it was understood in the earlier tradition. In that tradition the active life did not refer to apostolic activity but rather to the labors one undertook to overcome vice and acquire virtue so as to dispose oneself for contemplation.

3. This form of a threefold meditation, consideration of the past, present, and future, is common in Aelred. See below his *Pastoral Prayer*, n. 5, p. 110ff; *First Sermon for the Feast of the Annunciation*, n. 1; *First Sermon for the Feast of Pentecost*, n. 1; *Sermon Twenty-two on Isaiah*; etc. This form is also found frequently in Bernard of Clairvaux, see for example: *Third Sermon for the Sixth Sunday After Pentecost*, n. 6; *Occasional Sermons*, 12:1; *St Bernard's Five Books on Consideration*, Book 5, XIV, 32. We find other Cistercian

The Past

When your mind has been cleansed by the practice of the virtues from all the thoughts which clogged it, cast your eyes back, purified as they are now, to the past. First enter the room of blessed Mary and with her read the books which prophesy the virginal birth and the coming of Christ. Wait there for the arrival of the angel, so that you may see him as he comes in, hear him as he utters his greeting, and so, filled with amazement and rapt out of yourself, greet your most sweet Lady together with the angel. Cry with a loud voice: "Hail, full of grace, the Lord is with you, blessed are you among women."[4] Repeat this several times and consider what this fullness of grace is in which the whole world shared when the Word was made flesh and dwelt among us, full of grace and truth.[5] Wonder at the Lord who fills earth and heaven[6] being enclosed within the womb of a maiden, whom the Father sanctified, the Son fecundated and the Holy Spirit overshadowed.[7]

O sweet Lady, with what sweetness you were inebriated, with what a fire of love you were inflamed, when you felt in your mind and in your womb the presence of majesty, when he took flesh to himself from your flesh and fashioned for himself from your members members in which all the fullness of the Godhead might dwell in bodily form.[8] All this was on your account, virgin, in order

---

Fathers also using this form, e.g., Isaac of Stella, *On the Canon of the Mass*. It has a foundation in the tradition; see for example, St Ambrose, *On Cain and Abel*, XIII, 30; and it was developed by other contemporaries such as Grimlac, *Rule for Solitaries*, 29. See Dumont's consideration of this, *loc. cit.*, pp. 22f.

4. Lk 1:28.   5. Jn 1:14.   6. Jer 23:24.   7. Lk 1:35.

8. Col 2:9. It is a characteristic of the Cistercian authors, and indeed of the whole of medieval monastic writing, to break forth into prayer in the midst of discourses. As Dom Anselm LeBail has beautifully expressed it: "these men cannot maintain in their writings or in their sermons the uniquely didactic stance of the professor. They find it necessary to interrupt their exposition with prayers, with flights upward to God, with chants of praise. . . . Here perhaps we see the quintessence of the style of the Cistercian spirituality of the twelfth and thirteenth centuries. It is a search for God and the moment the insight is attained the heart bursts forth in chants of praise."—"La Spiritualité cistercienne," *Les Cahiers du Cercle Thomiste Fémine*, 7 (1927), p. 491.

that you might diligently contemplate the Virgin whom you have resolved to imitate and the Virgin's Son to whom you are betrothed.

But now together with your most sweet Lady go up into the mountains[9] and gaze upon the barren wife and the virgin as they embrace one another and exchange those greetings in which the little servant recognized and hailed with unspeakable joy his Lord, the herald recognized the Judge, the voice the Word, the one enclosed in the womb of his aged mother, the other confined in the Virgin's womb. Blessed the wombs in which the salvation of the whole world takes its origin, gloomy sadness is driven far away and everlasting joy foretold. What are you doing, virgin? Run, I beg, run and take part in such joy, prostrate yourself at the feet of both, in the womb of the one embrace your Bridegroom, in the womb of the other do honor to his friend.

Next with all your devotion accompany the Mother as she makes her way to Bethlehem. Take shelter in the inn with her, be present and help her as she gives birth, and when the infant is laid in the manger[10] break out into words of exultant joy[11] together with Isaiah and cry: "A child has been born to us, a son is given to us."[12] Embrace that sweet crib, let love overcome your reluctance, affection drive out fear.[13] Put your lips to those most sacred feet, kiss them again and again.

Next contemplate the shepherds' vigil, wonder at the angelic host, make your own contribution to their heavenly melody, singing both with your heart and with your lips: "Glory be to God on high, and on earth peace to men of good will."[14]

30. Do not omit the Magi and their gifts from your meditation, nor leave the Child unaccompanied on his flight into Egypt. Accept as true the legend that he was captured by robbers on the way and owed his escape to a young man who is supposed to have been the

---

9. Lk 1:39ff.　　　10. Lk 2:7.　　　11. Ps 41:5.　　　12. Is 9:6.

13. Aelred will come back upon this thought further on: n. 31, p. 86.

14. Lk 2:14. This paragraph has been cited by Rudolph the Carthusian in his *Vita Christi*, I, 9.

son of the robber chief.[15] After seizing his booty he looked at the Child in his Mother's bosom and was so impressed by the majesty that radiated from his beautiful face as to be convinced that he was something more than man. Inflamed with love he embraced him and said: "O most blessed of children, if ever the occasion arises to take pity on me, then remember me and do not forget the present moment." This is said to be the thief who was crucified at Christ's right hand and rebuked the other thief when he blasphemed. "What," he said, "have you no fear of God, when you are undergoing the same sentence? And we justly enough; we receive no more than the due reward of our deeds; but this man has done nothing amiss." Then, turning to our Lord and seeing in him that majesty which had distinguished him as a child, he remembered his agreement and said: "Remember me when you come into your kingdom."[16] So, in order to kindle love I consider it worthwhile to accept this legend as true, without making any rash assertions as to its authority.[17]

Further, do you not think you will gain some devotion by contemplating him at Nazareth as a boy among boys, obedient to his mother and helping his foster-father with his work?

31. Consider him too at the age of twelve going up to Jerusalem with his parents and staying in the city while they all unawares began their return. Join his Mother in looking for him during those three days. What a flood of tears will you not shed when you hear his Mother scolding her Son with the gentle reproach: "Son, why have you dealt so with us? Behold, your father and I have been looking for you in sorrow."[18]

If however you delight in following the Virgin wherever he

15. This is a legend from the *Arabic Infancy Gospels*, c. 23; see the *Apocryphal New Testament*, ed. M. R. James, p. 81.

16. Lk 23:40f.

17. Aelred is always careful to distinguish between what is a doctrine of faith or a clear teaching of Scripture and what pertains simply to the realm of opinion. Other examples of this can be seen in his *Second Sermon for the Feast of the Assumption*, n. 9, *Sermon Seventeen on Isaiah*, and above, *Jesus at the Age of Twelve*, n. 6, p. 10.

18. Lk 2:48.

goes[19] search out the depths that lie hidden in him. Thus at the river Jordan you will contemplate the Father in the voice, the Son in his human form, the Holy Spirit in the dove.[20] There, admitted to spiritual nuptials, you will gaze up at the Bridegroom given you by the Father, receiving the purification brought by the Son and the pledge of love from the Holy Spirit.

Next he dedicated for your benefit the solitude of the desert and sanctified fasting, to teach you that it is there you have to engage the crafty foe in battle.[21] Consider that this was done for you and in your stead; and meditate on the way in which it was done and imitate what was done.

Then call to mind the woman who was taken in adultery and what Jesus did and said when he was asked to give sentence, For he wrote on the earth, in order to show them up as of the earth rather than of heaven, and then said: "Let him among you who is without sin be the first to throw a stone at her."[22] But when the words struck them all with terror and drove them out of the temple imagine how kind were his eyes as he turned to her, how gentle and tender was the voice with which he pronounced his sentence of absolution. Think how he would have sighed, how he would have wept as he said: "Has no one condemned you, woman? Neither shall I condemn you."[23] Happy was the woman, I feel inclined to say, in this adultery, forgiven as she was for the past and assured for the future. Good Jesus, when it is you who say: "I will not condemn," who else will condemn? When it is God who justifies, who is there who will condemn?[24] Yet the words which you added must not be overlooked: "Go, and do not sin any more."[25]

Now go into the Pharisee's house and see our Lord in his place at table there.[26] Together with that most blessed sinner approach his feet, wash them with your tears, wipe them with your hair, soothe them with kisses and warm them with ointments. Are you not already penetrated with the fragrance of that sacred oil? If he still will not let you approach his feet, be insistent, beseech him, raise

19. Rev 14:4.   20. Lk 3:21f.   21. Lk 4:1ff.   22. Jn 8:3f.
23. Jn 8:10f.   24. Rom 8:33f.   25. Jn 8:11.   26. Lk 7:36.

G

your eyes to him brimming with tears and extort from him with deep sighs and unutterable groanings what you seek. Strive with God as Jacob did, so that he may rejoice in being overcome.[27] It will seem to you sometimes that he averts his gaze, closes his ears, hides the feet you long to touch. None the less be insistent, welcome or unwelcome, and cry out: "How long will you turn your face away from me?[28] How long shall I have to cry out without your listening to me?[29] Give back to me, good Jesus, the joy of your salvation,[30] for my heart has said to you: 'I have sought your face, your face, Lord, I will seek'."[31] He will certainly not refuse his feet to a virgin when he gave them to a sinful woman to kiss.

Do not pass by that house in which the paralytic was let down through the roof before his feet, where kindness and power came to meet one another. "My son," he said, "your sins are forgiven."[32] What amazing clemency, what unspeakable mercy. That happy man received forgiveness of his sins without having asked for it, without any preliminary confession, without having earned it by any satisfaction, without any contrition that might seem to call for it. It was bodily health he asked for, not that of the soul, yet he received health of both body and soul. Truly, Lord, life is at your disposal.[33] If you decide to save me, no one will be able to prevent you. If you decide otherwise no one will dare to say: "Why do you act so?"

Why do you complain, Pharisee? Is your eye evil because he is good?[34] Indeed he has mercy on whom he will.[35] Let us weep and pray that he may will. Let good works also help prayer to be more fervent, increase devotion, arouse love. Let the hands which are raised in prayer be pure, not stained with the blood of uncleanness, not soiled by unlawful touch, not polluted by avarice. Let the heart also which is lifted up be free from anger and quarrelling,[36] calm and tranquil, at peace, stirred to life by purity of conscience.

---

27. Gen 32:24ff. Aelred uses this same text to exemplify perseverence in prayer in *Sermon Fourteen on Isaiah.*

28. Ps 12:1. 29. Ps 21:3. 30. Ps 50:14. 31. Ps 26:8.
32. Mk 2:5. 33. Ps 29:6. 34. Mt 20:15. 35. Rom 9:18.
36. I Tim 2:8.

But we do not read that the paralytic had performed any of these preliminaries, and yet we read that he was found worthy to receive forgiveness of his sins. This is the power of Christ's unutterable mercy, and as it is blasphemous to deny it, so it is the height of folly to presume on it. He can say and do to anyone he wills the same as he said and did to the paralytic: "Your sins are forgiven,"[37] but anyone who expects this will be said to him without any toil or contrition or confession or even prayer on his part will never be forgiven his sins.

But we must leave this scene and come to Bethany, where the sacred bonds of friendship are consecrated by the authority of our Lord. For Jesus loved Martha, Mary and Lazarus.[38] There can be no doubt that this was on account of the special friendship by which they were privileged to be more intimately attached to him. That is borne out by those sweet tears with which he associated himself with the mourners and which all the people interpreted as a sign of love: "See," they said, "how he loved him."[39]

"And behold they gave him a supper there at which Martha was serving, while Lazarus was one of those at table with him. Now Mary brought ointment in an alabaster box and breaking the alabaster poured the ointment out upon Jesus' head."[40] Be glad, I beg of you, to take part in this meal. Mark carefully the part played by each of them. Martha was serving, Lazarus was reclining at table, Mary poured out ointment. This last function is for you. Break then the alabaster of your heart and whatever devotion you have, whatever love, whatever desire, whatever affection, pour it all out upon your Bridegroom's head, while you adore the man in God and God in the man.

If the traitor is indignant, if he complains and shows envy, if he calls your devotion waste, take no notice. "Why such waste?" he said, "this ointment could be sold for a high price and the money given to the poor."[41] The Pharisee complained because he grudged the penitent the grace she obtained. Judas complained because he

37. Mk 2:5.   38. Jn 11:5.   39. Jn 11:36.
40. Mk 14:3.   41. Mk 14:4f.

grudged the pouring out of the ointment. But the Judge did not admit the charge and absolved her against whom it was brought. "Let her be," he said, "she did well to treat me so.[42] Let Martha do her work, carry out her service, prepare accommodations for the pilgrim, food for the hungry, drink for the thirsty, clothes for the cold. I am wholly taken up with Mary and she with me; let her give me all that she has, let her expect to receive from me whatever she desires." What do you think? Surely you would not advise Mary to leave those feet which she is kissing so sweetly, or to turn her eyes away from that most beautiful face which she is contemplating, or to stop listening to the sweet words with which he regales her?

But now we must rise and go hence.[43] Where to? you ask. To be sure, to accompany the Lord of heaven and earth as he rides on an ass; to marvel at the great things which are done on your behalf and mingle your praise with that of the children, crying out: "Hosanna to the Son of David, blessed is he who comes in the name of the Lord."[44] Now then go up with him into the large upper room, furnished for supper,[45] and rejoice to share the delights of the meal which brings us salvation. Let love overcome shyness, affection drive out fear,[46] so that he may at least give you an alms from the crumbs of that table[47] when you beg for something. Or stand at a distance and, like a poor man looking to a rich man, stretch out your hand to receive something, let your tears declare your hunger. But when he rises from table, girds himself with the towel and pours water into the basin,[48] consider what majesty it is that is washing and drying the feet of men, what graciousness it is that touches with his sacred hands the feet of the traitor. Look and wait and, last of all, give him your own feet to wash, because the man whom he does not wash will have no part with him.[49]

Why are you in such a hurry to go out now? Wait a little while. Do you see? Who is that, I ask, who is reclining on his breast and bends back his head to lay it in his bosom?[50] Happy is he, whoever

42. Mk 14:6.   43. Jn 14:31.   44. Mt 21:9.   45. Mk 14:15.
46. See above for the same pastoral advice, n. 29, p.81.
47. Mt. 21:9.   48. Jn 13:5.   49. Jn 13:8.   50. Jn 13:25.

he may be. O, I see: his name is John.[51] O John, tell us what sweetness, what grace and tenderness, what light and devotion you are imbibing from that fountain. There indeed are all the treasures of wisdom and knowledge,[52] the fountain of mercy, the abode of loving kindness, the honeycomb of eternal sweetness. What have you done to deserve all this, John? Are you higher than Peter, more holy than Andrew, and more pleasing than all the other apostles? This is the special privilege of virginity: you were chosen to be a virgin by the Lord and therefore loved more than the rest.

Exult now, virgin, draw near and do not delay to claim for yourself some portion of this sweetness. If you are not capable of greater things, leave John to cheer himself with the wine of gladness in the knowledge of the Godhead[53] while you run to feed on the milk which flows from Christ's humanity.[54] Meanwhile when he commends his disciples to the Father in that most holy prayer and says: "Father, keep them in thy name,"[55] bow your head, so that of you too it may be said: "I wish that where I am they too may be with me."[56]

It is good for you to be here,[57] but we must depart. He himself leads the way to Mount Olivet, do you follow. And although, taking with him Peter and the two sons of Zebedee, he withdraws into solitude, look on if only from a distance and see how he takes

51. Lk 1:63.   52. Col 2:3.

53. In the tradition John is taken as a type of the contemplative. See for example, St Augustine, *Tracts on John*, 124:5; Bernard of Clairvaux, *Sermon Thirty-Three on the Song of Songs*, n. 9; Gilbert of Swineshead (who continued Bernard's commentary on the Song of Songs) *Sermons on the Song of Songs*, 12:3; 36:3.

54. The Cistercian Fathers frequently contrast these two forms of the knowledge of God. One through the humanity of Christ and the other through some experience of God as he is in himself. They do this especially in connection with Our Lord's words at the last supper: "It is expedient for you that I go," (Jn 16:7) and the words of his apostle Paul: "If we had known Christ according to the flesh, now we know him so no longer." (2 Cor 5:16). The need to begin with devotion to Christ's sacred humanity but then to pass on to the contemplation of the God-head is perhaps best developed by William of St Thierry in his *Exposition on the Song of Songs*, nn. 16ff., Cistercian Fathers Series 6, pp. 13ff.

55. Jn 17:11.   56. Jn 17:24.   57. Mt 17:4.

upon himself our weakness. See how he to whom everything belongs begins to be dismayed and afraid: "My soul is ready to die with sorrow,"[58] he says. How is this, my God? Your compassion for me makes you show yourself human to the extent that you seem almost to be no longer aware that you are God. You pray prostrate on your face and your sweat has become like drops of blood running down on to the ground.[59] Why are you standing there? Run up, consume those sweet drops and lick away the dust from his feet. Do not go to sleep with Peter, so that he will not have to say to you also: "Could you not then watch for one hour with me?"[60]

But here comes the traitor, followed by a crowd of the godless, and as Judas offers his kiss they lay their hands on your Lord.[61] They hold him, make him fast and tie those sweet hands with bonds. Who could endure such behavior? I know your heart now is filled with pity, you are set on fire with indignation. Let him be, I beg, let him suffer, for it is on your behalf he is suffering. Why do you long for a sword? Why are you angry? If, like Peter, you cut off someone's ear,[62] amputate an arm or a foot, he will restore it and without any doubt he will bring back to life anyone you may kill.

Follow him rather to the courtyard of the High Priest and bathe with your tears his most beautiful face which they are covering with spittle. See with what loving gaze, how mercifully, how effectually he looked at Peter who has thrice denied him and now turns, comes to his right mind and weeps bitterly.[63] Would that your sweet eyes, good Jesus, would look upon me who so often, at the voice of that insolent serving girl my flesh, have denied you by evil deeds and affections.

But now it is morning and he is delivered over to Pilate. There charges are brought against him and he says nothing,[64] because he is led to slaughter like a sheep, and like a lamb before the shearer he has not opened his mouth.[65] Mark well how he stands before the governor: his head bent, his eyes cast down, his face serene, saying

---

58. Mt 26:38.   59. Lk 22:44.   60. Mt 26:40.   61. Mt 26:47ff.
62. Mt 26:51.   63. Lk 22:61f.   64. Mt 26:63; Mk 14:61.
65. Is 53:7.

little, ready for insults and scourging. I know you can bear it no longer, that you will not be able to look on while his most sweet back is torn with whips, his face struck, his majestic head crowned with thorns, that right hand which made heaven and earth mocked with a reed.

See now, after the scourging he is led forth wearing the crown of thorns and the purple robe. Pilate says: "Behold the man."[66] Indeed he is a man. Who could doubt it? The weals left by the rods witness to it, the open wounds, the spittle which defiles him. Admit now, Satan, that this is a man. Indeed he is a man, you say. But why is it that, so outraged, he does not betray the anger which a man would show, does not rebel against his torturers as a man would? Therefore he is more than a man. But who knows him? He is known as a man to be sure as he undergoes the judgment of godless men, but as God he will be known when he himself comes to judge.[67]

You have realized it too late, Satan. What were you trying to do when you incited the woman to urge his release?[68] You have waited too long before speaking. The judge has taken his place at the judgment seat, the sentence has been pronounced and already the doomed man is led off to death carrying his own cross. O what a sight. Do you see? Behold princely power is upon his shoulder.[69] this is the sceptre of justice, the sceptre by which he reigns.[70] He is given wine mixed with gall. He is stripped of his garments and they are divided amongst the soldiers. The tunic is not torn but is given whole to the one designated by lot.[71] His sweet hands and feet are pierced with nails, he is stretched out on the Cross and hung up between two thieves. The Mediator of God and men[72] hangs midway between heaven and earth, unites the heights with the depths and joins the things of earth to the things of heaven. Heaven is aghast, earth marvels.

And what of you? It is not surprising if when the sun mourns you

---

66. Jn 19:5.   67. Ps 9:17.
68. The reference is to the wife of Pilate—see Mt 27:19.
69. Is 9:6.   70. Ps 44:7.   71. Jn 19:23f.   72. I Tim 2:5.

mourn too, if when the earth trembles you tremble with it, if when rocks are split your heart is torn in pieces, if when the women who are by the Cross weep you add your tears to theirs. However amid all this consider what tranquillity was preserved in that most sweet breast, what loving kindness it exhibited. He pays no attention to the wrongs done to him, takes no notice of the pain, disregards the insults, but rather has compassion on those who are making him suffer, heals those who are wounding him, wins life for those who are killing him. With what sweetness of disposition, with what devotion of spirit, in what fullness of charity he cries: "Father, forgive them."[73]

Here am I, Lord, adoring your majesty, not slaying your body, venerating your death, not mocking your passion, pondering your mercy, not despising your weakness. So may your sweet humanity intercede for me, may your unutterable loving kindness commend me to your Father. Say then, sweet Lord: "Father, forgive him." But you, virgin, who can feel more confidence with the Virgin's Son than the women who stand at a distance, draw near to the Cross with the Virgin Mother and the virgin disciple, and look at close quarters upon that face in all its pallor. What then? Will your eyes be dry as you see your most loving Lady in tears? Will you not weep as her soul is pierced by the sword of sorrow?[74] Will there be no sob from you as you hear him say to his Mother: "Woman, behold your son," and to John: "Behold your mother"?[75] Thus he entrusts his Mother to the disciple and also he promises the thief paradise.[76]

Then one of the soldiers opened his side with a lance and there came forth blood and water.[77] Hasten, linger not, eat the honeycomb with your honey, drink your wine with your milk.[78] The blood is changed into wine to gladden you, the water into milk to nourish you. From the rock streams have flowed for you,[79] wounds have been made in his limbs, holes in the wall of his body,[80]

---

73. Lk 23:34.   74. Lk 2:35.   75. Jn 19:26f.
76. Lk 23:43.   77. Jn 19:34.   78. Song 5:1.
79. Ps 77:16.   80. Song 2:14.

in which, like a dove, you may hide while you kiss them one by one. Your lips, stained with his blood, will become like a scarlet ribbon and your word sweet.[81]

But wait yet a while until that noble councilor[82] comes to extract the nails and free his hands and feet. See how in his most happy arms he embraces that sweet body and clasps it to his breast. Then could that holy man say: "My beloved is a bundle of myrrh for me, he shall rest upon my breast."[83] It is for you to follow that precious treasure of heaven and earth, and either hold the feet or support the hands and arms, or at least gather up carefully the drops of the precious blood as they fall one by one and wipe the dust from the feet. See also how gently, how solicitously blessed Nicodemus[84] handles his limbs, rubbing ointments on them, and then with holy Joseph wraps them in the shroud and lays them in the tomb.

Do not fail subsequently to keep Magdalen company, remember to visit with her your Lord's tomb, taking with you the perfumes she has prepared.[85] If only you might be found worthy to see in spirit what she saw with her eyes, now an angel sitting on the stone that has been rolled away from the entrance, now inside the tomb one angel where his head had lain, one where his feet, proclaiming the glory of his Resurrection, now Jesus himself looking with so gentle a gaze on Mary as she weeps for sorrow, and saying to her with so sweet a voice: "Mary."[86] What could be sweeter than this utterance? What could be more tender? What more delightful? "Mary." At this utterance let all the floods burst forth, let tears stream up from the very bottom of your heart, let sighs and sobs issue from your inmost depths. "Mary." O blessed one, what did you think, what did you feel, when you prostrated yourself at this utterance and answered his greeting with the cry: "Master"? With what affection, I ask, with what desire, with what fervor of mind and devotion of heart was it that you cried "Master"? Tears preclude any further utterance as the voice is stifled by emotion and excess of love leaves the soul dumb, the body without feeling.

81. Song 4:3.   82. Joseph of Arimathea. Mk 15:43.   83. Song 1:12.
84. Jn 19:39.   85. Lk 24:1ff.   86. Jn 20:16.

But, sweet Jesus, why do you keep at a distance from your most sacred feet her who in her love desires to clasp them? "Do not touch me,"[87] he says. What a harsh command, now intolerable: "Do not touch me." How is this, Lord? Why may I not touch you? May I not touch, may I not kiss those lovable feet, for my sake pierced with nails and drenched in blood? Are you less gentle than usual because you are more glorious? But I will not let you go,[88] I will not leave you, I will not spare my tears, my breast will burst with sobs and sighs unless I touch you.

His answer is: "Fear not, this boon is not refused you but kept until later. Only go and tell my brethren that I have risen."[89] She runs quickly, anxious to return quickly. She returns, but together with other women. These Jesus comes to meet with affection, restoring their spirits and banishing their sadness. And notice, the boon is now given which had previously been kept until later for they came close and clasped his feet.[90] Linger here as long as you can, virgin. Do not let these delights of yours be interrupted by sleep or disturbed by any tumult from without. However, since in this wretched life nothing is stable, nothing eternal, and man never remains in the same state,[91] our soul must needs, while we live, be fed with a certain variety. Therefore let us pass from the memory of what happened in the past to the experience of what is now present, so that it also may teach us how much we must love God.

The Present

32. I consider it to be no small benefit that he brought good out of the evil committed by our parents[92] and created us from their flesh, animating us with the breath of life[93] and setting us apart from

---

87. Jn 20:17.   88. Gen 32:26. See above n. 18, p. 67.
89. Jn 20:17.   90. Mt 28:9.   91. Job 14:2.

92. Aelred might be influenced here by the Augustinian doctrine according to which the marriage act was never free from sin. However, it is perhaps more probable that he is alluding here to the fact that he and his sister were the children of a married priest.

93. Cf. Alcher of Clairvaux, *On Loving God,* c. 9; PL 40:855.

those who were either ejected from the womb prematurely or stifled within the womb, conceived, it would seem, for punishment rather than for life. Then there is the fact that he created us with healthy, undeformed limbs and did not make us a burden to our family, an object of reproach to strangers. This is indeed a great benefit. But how highly shall we not price the gift of his goodness that we were born at a time and amid people that would enable us to come to his faith and his sacraments? Let us bear in mind that countless thousands of men have been denied what we rejoice to have been given; we share one and the same nature with them, yet they have been abandoned to the claims of justice while we have been called to receive grace.[94] Let us go on to realize that it was by his gift that we were brought up by our parents and not consumed by fire or drowned by waters or harassed by the devil or attacked by wild beasts or killed by falling from a height, in short that we were reared to a fitting age in his faith and good pleasure.

Up to this point, sister, we have run the same course, we were alike in everything: the same father begot us, the same womb bore us and gave us birth. But now let my life serve to bring out all that God has done for your soul.[95] For he separated you from me, as light from darkness,[96] keeping you for himself, leaving me to myself. My God, where did I go off to, where did I fly to, where did I abscond to? Indeed cast forth from your face like Cain I dwelt in the land of Nod, a wanderer and a fugitive, and whoever came across me killed me.[97] For what could a pitiable creature do once abandoned by its Creator? Where could a stray sheep go, where could it hide, when it had lost its shepherd?[98] Sister, a wild beast devoured your brother.[99] Let me serve then to show you how much he bestowed on you in keeping you unharmed by such a beast.

With my wretchedness then in the loss of my chastity compare your own happiness in the protection accorded to your virginity by God's grace. As often as you were tempted, as often as you were

---

94. *Ibid.*   95. Ps 65:16.   96. Gen 1:18.
97. Gen 4:14 (Septuagint) Cf. William of St Thierry, *On the Nature of Soul and Body*, n. 16, Cistercian Fathers Series 24.
98. 1 Pet 2:25.   99. Gen. 37:20.

attacked, your chastity remained inviolate, while I freely abandoned myself to all that is base, accumulating material for fire to burn me, for corruption to stifle me, for worms to gnaw me. Call to mind, if you will, my disgraceful behavior[100] on account of which you mourned for me and upbraided me often when we were young and after we had grown up. But Scripture is only telling the truth when it says: "No one can correct the man whom God abandons."[101] O how you ought to love him who drew you to himself while he repelled me, and, although we shared the same background, loved you but despised me.

Recall now, as I said, my corruption at the time when a cloud of passion exhaled from the murky depths of my fleshly desires and youthful folly, without anyone being at hand to rescue me.[102] The enticements of wicked men prevailed over me.[103] They gave me the poison of self-indulgence to drink in the sweet cup of love. The combination of innocent affection and impure desire beguiled my inexperience. I slid down the precipice of vice and was engulfed in the whirlpool of debauchery. Your anger and your indignation, God, weighed down upon me, and I did not know it. I withdrew further from you and you did not intervene. I was tossed about and utterly dissolute; I gave myself up to uncleanness, and you were silent.

Pay good heed, sister, to all this shameful and wicked behavior into which my own free will hurled me, and realize that you would have been in the same plight if Christ's mercy had not preserved you. I do not mean to say that he bestowed no good on me. To say nothing of the boons conferred on both of us alike, which I have already enumerated, he showed wonderful patience in bearing with my sins. Otherwise earth would have gaped open to swallow me, heaven's thunderbolts would have struck me down, rivers would have drowned me.[104] For how should creation endure such great wrong done to its Creator if its wrath were not held in check by

---

100. Cf. St Augustine, *Confessions,* 2, 1f.   101. Eccles 7:14.
102. Ps 7:3.   103. Ps 64:4.
104. Alcher of Clairvaux, *op. cit.,* c. 12.

that same Creator, who does not desire the death of the sinner but rather that he be converted and live?[105]

How generous was his grace in following me when I fled,[106] in allaying my fears, restoring me to hope as often as I was in despair, overwhelming my ingratitude with his kindnesses? I had grown accustomed to filthy pleasures and he drew me to himself and led me on by the taste of interior sweetness. He struck off the unbreakable shackles of bad habit. He rescued me from the world and welcomed me with kindness. I say nothing of the many and great works of his mercy towards me, lest any of the glory which belongs wholly to it should be deflected on to me. For in men's opinion the graciousness of the giver and the good fortune of the recipient are so connected that they praise not only him to whom alone praise is due, the giver, but also him who received the gift. What does a man possess that he has not received? And if he has received freely, why is he praised as if he had deserved the gift?[107] To you then, my God, belong praise, glory, thanksgiving;[108] to me, confusion for all the evil I have done and all the good I have received.

In what then, you ask, have you received less than me? O sister, how much more happy is the man whose ship, full of merchandise and loaded with riches, is brought to a safe homecoming by favorable winds than he who suffers shipwreck and barely escapes death with the loss of all?[109] So you exult in these riches which God's grace has preserved for you, while I have the utmost difficulty in repairing what has been broken, recovering what has been lost, mending what has been torn. Yet in this respect I would have you emulate me. How you would have to blush if after all my sins I were found equal to you in the next life. The glory of virginity is often

---

105. Ezek 33:11.   106. Alcher of Clairvaux, *op. cit.*, c. 15.

107. 1 Cor 4:7.

108. Cistercian Breviary, Antiphon for Tierce, Feast of the Most Holy Trinity.

109. St Gregory the Great, *Homily Thirty-seven on Ezechiel;* Alcher of Clairvaux, *Mirror*, c. 30; PL 40:981.

tarnished by vices which make their way in later on, while the re-
formation of a man's life and the replacement of vices by virtues
can cancel the infamy of his former behavior.

But now consider those gifts of God's goodness which are known
only to yourself. With how glad a face Christ comes to meet one
who renounces the world, with what delights he feeds her in her
hunger, what riches of his compassion he shows her, what affections
he arouses in her, with what a cup of charity he inebriates her.[110]
For if he did not leave his runaway and rebellious slave, called solely
in his mercy, without the experience of spiritual consolations, what
sweetness shall I not believe he bestowed on a virgin? If you were
tempted he supported you; if you were in danger, he raised you up;
if you were downcast, he comforted you; if you were carried this
way and that he brought you stability. How often he came to your
side to bring you loving consolation when you were dried up by
fear, how often he infused himself into your inmost being when you
were on fire with love, how often he shed upon you the light of
spiritual understanding when you were singing psalms or reading,
how often he carried you away with a certain unspeakable longing
for himself when you were at prayer, how often he lifted up your
mind from the things of earth and introduced it into the delights of
heaven and the joys of Paradise.

Turn all this over in your mind, so that your spirit may go out
wholly to him. Let the world become of no value to you, let all
carnal love seem defiled. Forget that you are in this world, because
you have shifted your interest to those who are in heaven and live
for God. Where your treasure is, there let your heart also be.[111] Do
not shut up your spirit with silver images in your worthless purse,
for it will never be able to wing its flight to heaven if it is weighed
down by coins. Consider that each day will be your last and then
you will have no thought for the morrow; do not be frightened by
the drought or cast down by fear of the famine that lie in the future,
but put all your trust in him who feeds the birds and clothes the

110. Cf. Alcher of Clairvaux, *On Loving God,* c. 15.
111. Mt 6:21.

lilies.[112] Let him be your barn, your storecupboard, your purse, your wealth, your delight; let him alone be all things in all.[113]

Let this be enough for the time being of present things.

The Future

33. But if such are the gifts he bestows on his own in the present, what must be those he is keeping for them in the future?

The beginning of the future and the end of the present is death. Is there anyone who has not a natural repulsion for death, who does not feel a dread of it? Wild beasts guard themselves from death, preserve life by flight, hiding-places and a thousand other devices.[114] Now then examine yourself carefully. What answer does your conscience give you, what is it your faith counts on, your hope promises you, your affections expect.

If your life is a burden to you, if you are weary of the world, if the flesh brings you only pain, then indeed death is something you long for, to free you from the burden of this life, to put an end to your weariness, to take away bodily pain. This by itself I consider to surpass all the delights of this world, all its honors and riches: to have such serenity of conscience, such firm faith and such certain hope that you do not fear death.[115] Some experience of this will come especially to the man who on occasion, sighing under the burden of his servitude, has been enabled to breathe the fresh air of a conscience set at liberty.[116] These are the wholesome first fruits of your beatitude to come, so that at the moment of death the natural horror you feel for it may be overcome by faith, softened by hope, driven away by an assured conscience.

Consider too how death is the beginning of eternal happiness, the goal of all your labors, the destroyer of vice. For so it is written: "Blessed are the dead who die in the Lord. Let them rest from their

---

112. Mt 6:26f.   113. Eph 1:23; Col 3:11.

114. See Aelred's *Treatise on the Soul*, Bk. 1.

115. Cf. *Mirror of Charity*, 1:28.

116. Cf. *Mirror of Charity*, 1:21. See also Dumont, *Sources Chrétiennes* 76, p. 29, especially note 2.

labors, says the Spirit."[117] Therefore the Prophet distinguishes between the death of the reprobate and that of the elect in the words: "All the kings have fallen asleep in glory, each in his own house, while you have been cast out of your tomb like a useless root, twisted and decayed."[118] They indeed sleep in glory whose death is commended by a good conscience, for in the eyes of the Lord the death of his saints is precious.[119] Truly he sleeps in glory whose falling asleep is attended by angels, whom saints come to meet, bringing help and solace to their fellow-citizen and withstanding his enemies, driving off those who stand in the way, repelling those who bring charges against him, and so accompanying his holy soul right up to Abraham's bosom and depositing it in a place of peace and rest.

Not so is it with the wicked, not so.[120] Evil spirits with the instruments of hell drag them from the body as from a fetid tomb and cast them, defiled with lust, wrapped up in covetousness, into fire to burn. They commit them to worms to be gnawed, deliver them up to be stifled by eternal stench. Indeed the expectation of the just is gladness, while the hope of the godless shall perish.[121]

As for that rest, that peace, that enjoyment in Abraham's bosom[122] that is promised to those who rest there and is looked for by them, because no experience has taught us what it is like no pen can describe it. Those happy souls are waiting until the number of their brethren is complete, in order that on the day of the resurrection, clad in the glory of the twofold robe,[123] they may enjoy unending happiness of body and soul alike.

But now turn your gaze to the terror of that day when the powers of heaven will be moved,[124] the elements dissolved in the heat of fire, when hell will gape open and all that is hidden will be laid bare.[125] From on high the Judge will come in anger, his fury all ablaze and his chariot like a storm. In his wrath he will exact vengeance and lay waste with flaming fire. Blessed is the man who is ready to meet him. What will be the plight then of the wretches

---

117. Rev 14:13.   118. Is 14:19.   119. Ps 115:15.
120. Ps 1:4.   121. Prov 10:28.   122. Lk 16:22.
123. Rev. 6:11.   124. Mk 13:25.   125. 1 Cor 14:25.

who are now defiled by lust, dissipated by avarice, lifted up by pride? The angels will go forth and separate the wicked from the midst of the just, setting these on the right and the others on the left.[126]

Imagine now that you are standing before Christ's judgment-seat between these two companies and have not yet been assigned to one or the other. Turn your eyes to the left of the Judge and gaze upon that wretched multitude. What horror is there, what a stench, what fear, what grief? They stand there miserable and unhappy, gnashing their teeth, their bare flesh shaking with fear, dreadful to look upon, their faces distorted, cast down from shame, in confusion because of their body's degradation and nakedness. They want to hide and they are not allowed, they try to flee and it is not granted them. If they raise their eyes the Judge's fury bears down upon them from above. If they lower them they are filled with the horror of hell's pit. They have no excuse to offer for their crimes nor is there any chance of claiming that the judgment is unfair, since whatever is decided their own conscience will recognize as just.

See now how you should love him who has set you apart from this doomed company by his predestination, separated you by his call, cleansed you by his justification.[127] Now turn your eyes to the right and look at those among whom he will place you by glorifying you. What grace is there, what honor, what happiness, what security. Some take their seat on high to give judgment, some are resplendent in martyrs' crowns, some are bearing the white flower of virginity, some display the fruit of almsgiving, some are illustrious for their doctrine and their learning, but they are all united by the bond of charity. Jesus' face shines upon them, not terrible but lovable, not bitter but sweet, not frightening but attractive.

Now stand in the middle, not knowing to which company the Judge's sentence will assign you. O what a dreadful waiting. Fear and trembling have come upon me and darkness has covered me.[128] If he sends me to join those on the left I cannot complain of injustice; if he sets me among those on the right it is to be attributed

126. Mt 13:49; 25:33. 127. Rom 8:30. 128. Ps 54:6.

H

to his grace, not to my merits. Truly, Lord, life is at your disposal.[129] You see then how your spirit should be absorbed in his love.

Although in all justice he could have extended to you the sentence passed on the wicked, he preferred to place you among those who are to be saved.

Now imagine yourself associated with that holy company and hearing his voice utter the decree: "Come, ye blessed of my Father, receive the kingdom which was prepared for you from the beginning of the world,"[130] while those other wretched souls hear the harsh words, full of anger and fury: "Depart from me, ye accursed, into eternal fire."[131] "Then," we read, "they will go to eternal punishment, but the just to eternal life."[132] What a harsh separation, what a miserable lot.

When the wicked have been removed, lest they should see the glory of God, and each of the just has taken his place according to his rank and his merits in the orders of the angels, that glorious procession will be formed, Christ our Head in the front, followed by all his members. Then the kingdom will be delivered to God the Father in order that he may reign over them and they may reign with him, receiving that kingdom which was prepared for them from the beginning of the world.

What that kingdom will be like we cannot even think, let alone say or write.[133] But this I know, that nothing at all will be missing that you would wish to be there, and nothing will be there that you would wish not to be. So there will be no mourning, no weeping or pain, no fear, no sadness,[134] no discord, no envy, no tribulation, no temptation, no variable weather, no overcast skies, no suspicion, no ambition, no adulation, no detraction, no sickness, no old age, no death, no poverty, no darkness, no need to eat, drink or sleep, no tiredness, no weakness.

---

129. Ps 29:6.   130. Mt 25:34.   131. Mt 25:41.   132. Mt 25:46.

133. In this paragraph we see a close relationship between Aelred and John of Fécamp, *Liber Meditationum,* c. 21 (PL 40:917); *Soliloquum Animae ad Deum,* c. 35 (PL 40:895) and also Alcher of Clairvaux, *On Loving God,* c. 18 (PL 40:862f.).

134. Rev. 21:4.

What good then will be lacking? Where there is no mourning or weeping or pain or sadness, what can there be but perfect joy? Where there is no tribulation or temptation, no variable weather or overcast skies, no excessive heat or harsh winter, what can there be but perfect balance in all things and complete tranquillity of mind and body? Where there is nothing to fear, what can there be but total security? Where there is no discord, no envy, no suspicion or ambition, no adulation or detraction, what can there be but supreme and true love? Where there is no poverty and no covetousness, what can there be but abundance of all good things? Where there is no deformity, what can there be but true beauty? Where there is no toil or weakness, what will there be but utter rest and strength? Where there is nothing heavy or burdensome, what is there but the greatest ease? Where there is no prospect of old age, no fear of disease, what can there be but true health? Where there is neither night nor darkness, what will there be but perfect light? Where all death and mortality have been swallowed up,[135] what will there be but eternal life?

What is there further for us to seek? To be sure, what surpasses all these things, that is the sight, the knowledge and the love of the Creator. He will be seen in himself, he will be seen in all his creatures, ruling everything without anxiety, upholding everything without toil, giving himself and, so to speak, distributing himself to one and all according to their capacity without any lessening or division of himself. That lovable face, so longed for, upon which the angels yearn to gaze,[136] will be seen. Who can say anything of its beauty, of its light, of its sweetness? The Father will be seen in the Son, the Son in the Father, the Holy Spirit in both. He will be seen not as a confused reflection in a mirror, but face to face.[137] For he will be seen as he is,[138] fulfilling that promise which tells us: "He who loves me will be loved by my Father, and I will love him and show myself to him."[139] From this vision will proceed that knowledge of which he says again: "This is eternal life, that they should know you the one God, and him whom you sent,

135. 1 Cor 15:54.   136. 1 Pet 1:12.   137. 1 Cor 13:12.
138. 1 Jn 3:2.   139. Jn 14:21.

Jesus Christ."[140] Hence there is born such love, such ardent affection, such sweetness of charity, such abundance of enjoyment, such vehement desire, that neither does satiety lessen desire nor desire hinder satiety.[141] What is this? To be sure, what eye has not seen nor ear heard, nor heart conceived, what God has prepared for those who love him.[142]

Conclusion

These, sister, are some seeds of spiritual meditation which I have made it my business to sow for you concerning the memory of Christ's boons in the past, the experience of things present and the expectation of what lies in the future, to the end that from them a rich crop of the love of God may spring up and grow to maturity. Meditation will arouse the affections, the affections will give birth to desire,[143] desire will stir up tears, so that your tears may be bread for you day and night[144] until you appear in his sight and say to him what is written in the Song of Songs: "My Beloved is mine and I am his."[145]

You have now what you asked for: rules for bodily observances by which a recluse may govern the behavior of the outward man; directions for cleansing the inner man from vices and adorning him with virtues; a threefold meditation to enable you to stir up the love of God in yourself, feed it and keep it burning.

If anyone makes any progress as a result of reading this little book, let her make me this return for my toil and my care, to intercede for my sins with my Savior whom I await, with my Judge whom I fear.

THE END OF THE BOOK ON THE RULE OF LIFE FOR RECLUSES.

---

140. Jn 17:3.
141. Cf. St Augustine, *Sermon Three Hundred and Sixty-two*, 28, 29 (PL 39:1633); St Gregory the Great, *Homilies on the Gospel*, II, 36, 1 (PL 76:1266).
142. 1 Cor 2:9.
143. This passage up to this point is quoted by Ludolph of Saxony in his *Vita Christi*, II, 89.
144. Ps 41:4.   145. Song 2:16.

HERE BEGINS
THE PASTORAL PRAYER
OF THE VENERABLE AELRED,
ABBOT OF RIEVAULX,
A PRAYER COMPOSED AND
REGULARLY USED BY HIM
AND APT FOR THOSE WHO ARE
SET OVER OTHERS,
ABBOTS ESPECIALLY

Address

1.
                O Good Shepherd Jesus,[1]
            good, gentle, tender Shepherd,
        behold a shepherd, poor and pitiful,
        a shepherd of your sheep indeed,[2]
        but weak and clumsy and of little use,
                cries out to you.
        To you, I say, Good Shepherd,
    this shepherd, who is not good, makes his prayer.
                He cries to you,
    troubled upon his own account,[3] and troubled for your
                    sheep.

1. Jn 10:11ff. Dom André Wilmart has pointed out a number of parallel
between this *Pastoral Prayer* of Aelred and the one attributed to St Anselm:
Oratio 75; PL 158:1012ff.

2. Jn 21:17.   3. Ps 101:1f.

Act of Contrition

2.   For when in bitterness of soul
                            I view my former life,[4]
it scares and frightens me that I should be called shepherd,
    for I am surely crazy if I do not know myself
                    unworthy of the name.
                Your holy mercy is upon me,
    to snatch my wretched soul out of the nether hell.[5]
                You show mercy as you will;[6]
your pity succours him whom you are pleased to pity;[7]
        and such is your forgiveness of my sin,
    that you do not avenge yourself by damning me,
    nor do you even overwhelm me with reproaches;
and, even when you do accuse, you love me no less.
        Nevertheless, I am disturbed and troubled,
        for I am mindful of your goodness, yes—
    but I am not unmindful of my own ingratitude.
                        See, then,
before you is my heart's confession of the countless sins,
from which your mercy has been pleased to free my
                        hapless soul.
    My whole heart renders thanks and praise to you[8]
        with all its might for all these benefits.
            But I am no less in your debt
        for all the evil things I have not done.
        For, most assuredly, whatever evil thing
        I have not done, it was your guiding hand
            that made me abstain from doing it;
    since either you did take away the means thereto,
        or else you did correct my inclination,
            or gave me the power to resist.

4. See above *Rule of Life for a Recluse*, n. 32, pp. 93f.
5. Ps 85:13.   6. Ex 33:19.   7. Rom 9:15.   8. Jer 31:20.

But what am I to do, O Lord my God,
about the ills whereby, in your just judgment,
you suffer your servant, the son of your handmaiden,[9]
still to be wearied and be overcome?
The things concerning which my sinful soul
is troubled in your sight, O Lord, cannot be counted;
yet, for all that,
neither my sorrow for them nor my care
to shun their repetition is as great
as they demand, and as my will desires.

Facing His Office

3.   To you, my Jesus, I confess, therefore;
to you, my Savior and my hope,
to you, my comfort and my God, I humbly own
that I am not as contrite and as fearful as I ought to be
for my past sins;
nor do I feel enough concern about my present ones.
And you, sweet Lord,
have set a man like this over your family,[10]
over the sheep of your pasture.[11]
Me, who take all too little trouble with myself,
you bid to be concerned on their behalf;
and me,
who never pray enough about my own sins,
you would have pray for them.
I, who have taught myself so little too,
have also to teach them.
Wretch that I am, what have I done?
What have I undertaken?
What was I thinking of?

9. Ps 115:16 (Vulgate).   10. Mt 24:35.   11. Ps 71:1; 78:13.

Or rather, sweetest Lord, what were you thinking of
regarding this poor wretch?
Sweet Lord, I pray you, is not this your family,[12]
your own peculiar people,[13] that has been led by you
out of the second Egypt,[14] and by you has been
created and redeemed?
And lastly, you have gathered them together
out of all parts, and made them live together[15]
in a house where all men follow a common way of life.[16]
Why then, O font of mercy, have you willed
to put such people, souls so dear to you
into the charge of such an outcast from your face?[17]
Was it to satisfy my appetites, to give free rein to my
desires,[18]
in order that you might have the more against me,
and sentence me with more severity,
and punish me for others' sins, as well as for my own?[19]
O God most holy, if this were the case,
was it then fair to let so many souls, souls of such quality,
suffer such risk, solely that there might be
more obvious reason for one man's severer punishment?
For to what greater peril can subjects be exposed,
than to a stupid and sinful superior?
Or—and this it is more seemly to expect,
more pleasant to experience from kindness such as yours—
did you set such a person over your household, Lord,
in order that, if it should please your goodness
to rule it well through him,

---

12. Mt 24:45.   13. Deut 7:6.

14. Ps 80:11. In an imagery which was common among monastic writers,
Egypt was a type of the world and the monastic community was the chosen
people of God who under the new Moses, St Benedict, were being led to the
promised land having left the world (Egypt) through monastic conversion.
See for example Aelred's *First* and *Third Sermons for the Feast of St Benedict*,
Cistercian Fathers Series 23.

15. Ps 106:2.   16. Ps 67:2.   17. Ps 30:23.
18. Rom 1:24.   19. Ps 18:14.

your mercy might be shown, your wisdom known,[20]
the excellence of your power declared thereby
as yours alone, not man's;[21]
and so the wise, the righteous, and the strong
should never glory in their wisdom, righteousness and
strength
as though they were their own;[22]
for, when such persons rule your people well,
it is not they, but you, that rule them.
Give not the glory unto us, O Lord, if this be so,
but unto your own name.[23]

Introduction to the Prayers that Follow

4.　　　Yet, Lord, whatever be the reason why
you have put my unworthy, sinful self
into this office, or have suffered others
to appoint me to it,
the fact remains that you command me
—so long as you allow me to hold the same—
to be concerned for those set under me,
and to pray for them most particularly.
Wherefore, O Lord,
I lay my prayers before you, trusting not
in my own righteousness, but in your great mercy;[24]
and where no merit of my own can lift its voice,
duty is eloquent.
Let your eyes, therefore, be upon me, Lord,
and let your ears be open to my prayers.[25]
But since, according to the law divine,
a priest is bound to offer sacrifice

20. Ps 105:8.　　　21. 2 Cor 4:7.　　　22. Jer 9:23.
23. Ps 113:9.　　　24. Dan 9:18.　　　25. Ps 33:16.

first for himself, thereafter for his people,[26]
I make oblation to your majesty
first of the sacrifice of prayer for my own sins.

Prayer for his own Needs

5.   Lord, look at my soul's wounds.
Your living and effective eye sees everything.[27]
It pierces like a sword, even to part asunder soul and
spirit.[28]
Assuredly, my Lord, you see in my soul
the traces of my former sins,
my present perils,
and also motives and occasions for others yet to be.
You see these things, Lord,
and I would have you see them.
You know well, O Searcher of my heart,[29]
that there is nothing in my soul that I would hide from
you,
even had I the power to escape your eyes.
Woe to the souls that want to hide themselves from
you.[30]
They cannot make themselves not to be seen by you,
but only miss your healing and incur your punishment.
So see me, sweet Lord, see me.
My hope, most Merciful, is in your loving kindness;
for you will see me, either as a good physician sees,
intent upon my healing,
or else as a kind master, anxious to correct,
or a forbearing father, longing to forgive.

26. Lev 9:7; Heb 5:3.   27. Sir 23:27.   28. Heb 4:12.
29. Prov 24:12.   30. Is 29:15.

This, then, is what I ask, O font of pity,
trusting in your mighty mercy and merciful might:
I ask you, by the power of your most sweet name,
and by your holy manhood's mystery,
to put away my sins and heal the languors of my soul,
mindful only of your goodness, not
of my ingratitude.
Further, against the vices and the evil passions
which still assault my soul,
(whether they come from past bad habit, or
from my immeasurable daily negligence,
whether their source is in the weakness
of my corrupt and vitiated nature,
or in the secret tempting of malignant spirits)
against these vices, Lord, may your sweet grace
afford me strength and courage;
that I may not consent thereto, nor let them reign
in this my mortal body,
nor yield my members to be instruments of wickedness.[31]
And as I thus resist,
do you the while heal all my weakness perfectly,
cure all my wounds, and put back into shape
all my deformities.
Lord, may your good, sweet Spirit[32]
descend into my heart,
and fashion there a dwelling for himself,[33]
cleansing it from all defilement both of flesh and spirit,[34]
impouring into it the increment of faith, and hope,
and love,
disposing it to penitence and love and gentleness.

---

31. Rom 6:12f.   32. Ps 142:10.   33. Ps 32:14.

34. 2 Cor 7:1. Here we can see a parallel between Aelred's *Pastoral Prayer* and that of John Fécamp (found among the prayers of St Anselm, *Prayer Twenty-nine*; PL 158:924).

May he quench with the dew of his blessing
the heat of my desires,
and with this power put to death
my carnal impulses and fleshly lusts.[35]
In labors, and in watchings, and in fastings
may he afford me fervor and discretion,
to love and praise you, to pray and think of you;
and may he give me power and devotion
to order every act and thought according to your will,
and also perseverance in these virtues
unto my life's end.

Special Prayer for Wisdom

6.   These things, my Hope,
I need for my own sake.
But there are others that I need
not only for myself, but for the sake of those
to whom you bid me be a power for good,
rather than merely a superior.[36]
There was a wise king once, who asked
that wisdom might be given him to rule your people.[37]
His prayer found favor in your eyes,
you did hearken thereto;
and at that time you had not met the Cross,
nor shown your people that amazing love.
But now, sweet Lord, behold before your face
your own peculiar people, whose eyes are ever on your
Cross,
and who themselves are signed with it.
You have entrusted to your sinful servant
the task of ruling them.
My God, you know what a fool I am,

35. *Ibid.*, PL 158:921f.   36. RB 64:8.   37. 2 Chron 1:10.

my weakness is not hidden from your sight.[38]
Therefore, sweet Lord, I ask you not for gold,
I ask you not for silver, nor for jewels,
but only that you would give me wisdom,
that I may know to rule your people well.
O font of wisdom, send her from your throne of might,
to be with me, to work with me,[39]
to act in me, to speak in me,
to order all my thoughts and words and deeds and plans
according to your will,
and to the glory of your name,
to further their advance and my salvation.

Prayer for the Good of All

7.   You know my heart, Lord;
You know that my will is
that whatever you have given your servant
should be devoted wholly to their service,
and spent for them in its entirety;
and I myself, moreover, would be freely spent for them.[40]
So may it be, O Lord, so may it be.
My powers of perception and of speech,
my work time and my leisure,
my doing and my thinking,
the times when things go well with me,
the times when they go ill,
my life, my death,
my good health and my weakness,
each single thing that makes me what I am,
the fact that I exist and think and judge,
let all be used, let all be spent for those

---

38. Ps 68:6.   39. Wis 9:10.   40. 2 Cor 12:15.

for whom you did deign to be spent yourself.
Teach me your servant, therefore, Lord,
teach me, I pray you, by your Holy Spirit,
how to devote myself to them and how
to spend myself on their behalf.
Give me, by your unutterable grace, the power
to bear with their shortcomings patiently,
to share their griefs in loving sympathy,
and to afford them help according to their needs.
Taught by your Spirit may I learn
to comfort the sorrowful, confirm the weak and raise
the fallen;
to be myself one with them in their weakness,
one with them when they burn at causes of offence,[41]
one in all things with them, all things to all of them,
that I may gain them all.[42]
Give me the power to speak the truth straightforwardly,
and yet acceptably;
so that they all may be built up in faith and hope and love,
in chastity and lowliness, in patience and obedience,
in spiritual fervor and submissiveness of mind.
And, since you have appointed this blind guide to lead
them,[43]
this untaught man to teach, this ignorant one to rule
them,[44]
for their sakes, Lord, if not for mine,
teach him whom you have made to be their teacher,
lead him whom you have bidden to lead them,
rule him who is their ruler.
Teach me, therefore, sweet Lord,
how to restrain the restless, comfort the discouraged,

---

41. 1 Cor 9:19; 2 Cor 11:29.   42. 1 Cor 9:22.   43. Mt 15:14.

44. *Caecum ductorem, indoctum doctorem, nescium rectorem*—a beautiful passage which calls to mind St Gregory's description of St Benedict in the Prologue to the 2 bk. of the *Dialogues: scienter nescius et sapienter indoctus.*

and support the weak.[45]

Teach me to suit myself to everyone

according to his nature, character and disposition,

according to his power of understanding or his lack of it,

as time and place require, in each case,

as you would have me do.

And since the weakness of my flesh[46]

—or it may be my lack of courage and my heart's

corruption[47]—

prevent my edifying them by labours of watching and

fasting,

I beg your bounteous mercy that they may be edified

by my humility and charity, my patience and my pity.

May my words and teaching build them up,

and may they always be assisted by my prayers.

Prayer for Subordinates

8.   Hear me yet further, God most merciful,

for those for whom I am compelled and drawn to pray

to you

both by my duty and by my heart's love.

Remembering your kindness, I am bold.

For you, sweet Lord, know how much I love them,

how I yearn over them, and how my heart goes out to

them.[48]

You know, Lord,

I do not want to rule them harshly or self-assertively, [49]

but to help them in charity, rather than command,[50]

and to be subject to them in humility,

while being always one of them in sympathy.

45. 1 Thes 5:14.   46. Rom 6:19; Gal 4:13.   47. Ps 54:9.
48. Job 16:14.   49. Ez 34:4.   50. RB 64:8.

I

Hear me, therefore, hear me, O Lord my God,[51]
and let your eyes be open on them day and night.[52]
Spread your wings,[53] most loving Lord and shield them
stretch forth your holy right hand, Lord, and bless them;
and pour into their hearts your Holy Spirit,
that he may keep them in unity of spirit and the bond of
peace,[54]
chaste in their bodies, lowly in their minds.
May he be there to help them when they pray,
and fill them with the unction and the riches of your
love.[55]
May he renew their minds with sweet compunction,
enlighten their hearts with the light of your grace
cheer them with hope and humble them with fear,
and kindle them with love.
May it be he who prompts them to such prayers
as you will gladly hear.
May he, your same sweet Spirit, be in them,
when they make meditation;
so that, by him enlightened, they may know you,
and ever cherish in their hearts the thought of him;
so that in trouble they will call on him,
and turn to him in all perplexity.
May the same loving Comforter, when they are being
tempted,
come swiftly to their aid;
and may he help their weakness in all the
straits and troubles of this life.
By the same Spirit make them, Lord, to be,
within themselves, with one another, and towards
myself
peaceable and equable and kind,

---

51. 1 Sam 18:37.   52. 1 Sam 8:29.   53. Deut 32:11.
54. Cistercian Missal, the Prayer to be said during the General Chapter.
55. Eph 4:3.

obedient,[56] servicable,[57] helpful, to each other.[58]

May they be fervent in spirit, rejoicing in hope,[59]

enduring steadfastly[60]

through poverty and fasting, toils and vigils,[61] silence and repose.

Drive far from them, O Lord, the spirit

of pride and of vain glory,

of envy and of gloom,

of weariness[62] and slander,

of distrust and despair,

of fornication and uncleanness,

of discord and presumption.

Be in their midst, according to your faithful promise.[63]

And, since you know what each of them needs,

I pray you, strengthen what is weak in them.[64]

spurn not their frailty, heal that which is diseased,

give joy for sorrow, kindle what is lukewarm,

establish what is insecure in them, that each of them may

know he does not lack your grace in any of his trials and temptations.

Prayer for Temporal Needs

9.   Lord, as you shall see fit,

provide your servants also with those temporal goods

whereby the weakness of this wretched body

is in this life sustained.

This one thing only do I crave, my Lord,

from your sweet pity:

56. Ps 62:6; RB 71.   57. RB 35:1.   58. Col 3:13.
59. Rom 12:11f.   60. 1 Thes 5:14.   61. 2 Cor 6:5.
62. *Acedia*—see above, *Jesus at the Age of Twelve*, n. 24, note 29, p. 31.
63. Mt 18:20.   64. Ezek 34:4.

namely, that whether it be much or little that you give
you would make me, your servant,
a good and faithful steward in respect to all,[65]
a wise and fair distributor,
a sensible provider.
Inspire them too, my God, to bear it patiently
when you withhold things;
and, when you do bestow, to use your gifts
with temperance and restraint.
Inspire them, O Lord, also to have of me,
who am your servant, and their servant for your sake,
such an opinion as may profit them,
such love and fear of me,[66]
as you, Lord, see to be good for them.

Conclusion

10.   I, for my part, commit them
into your holy hands and loving providence.
May no one snatch them from your hand,[67]
nor from your servant's, unto whom you have committed
them.
May they persevere with gladness in their holy purpose,
unto the attainment of everlasting life
with you, our most sweet Lord, their Helper always,
who live and reign to ages of ages. Amen.

65. Lk 12:42.

66. RB 64:15. It is clear from Aelred's use of Ezek 34, Jn 10, *Dialogues* 2 and RB 64 that he intends to coalesce the ideals of Christ the Good Shepherd and St Benedict's Father Abbot into a single synthesis with his own shortcomings brought forward as a foil.

67. Jn 10:28. The Editors would like to express their gratitude to Dom Alberic Stacpoole osb for his kindness in looking over the manuscript and for the helpful suggestions he made.

SELECT BIBLIOGRAPHY

I. SOURCES AND TRANSLATIONS

From its appearance in March, 1971, the ruling source for St Aelred's spiritual works must be—

Hoste, A. and Talbot, C. H., ed., *Aelredi Rievallensis Opera Omnia,* 1: *Opera Ascetica,* (hereafter Aelred Opera 1), *Corpus Christianorum, Continuatio Medievalis* 1, Steenbrugge, Turnholt.

a. Jesus at the Age of Twelve

Hoste, A., ed., *De Jesu Puero Duodenni,* Aelred Opera 1:249–78, textus criticus (as below).
Quand Jésus eut Douze Ans, Sources Chrétiennes 60 (1958). Introduction and Latin text, French transl. J. Dubois.

Webb, G. and Walker, A., *On Jesus at Twelve Years Old* (1956). English transl.
Early mss ascribed this work to St Bernard. It is in Mabillon, *Bernardi Opera* II (1690), 577–90 and Migne PL 184:849–70.

b. A Rule of Life for a Recluse

Talbot, C. H., ed., *De Institutione Inclusarum,* Aelred Opera 1:637–82, textus criticus as in *Analecta Sacr. Ord. Cist.* 7 (1951), 167–217.

Dumont, C. ed., *La Vie de Recluse,* Sources Chrétiennes 76
(1961), 40–169. Introduction and Latin
text, French transl.

Webb, G. and Walker, A., *A Letter to his Sister* (1957).
English transl. omitting the
first twenty chapters.

Early mss ascribed this work to St Augustine and to St
Anselm. It is therefore in Migne twice, PL 32:1451–74
and PL 158:785–94.

c. The Pastoral Prayer

Wilmart, A., ed. *Oratio Pastoralis,* Aelred Opera 1:757–63,
textus criticus as in *Revue Bénédictine* 37
(1925), 263–72, emended *ib.* 41 (1929),
74.

Dumont, C., ed., *La Prière Pastorale,* Sources Chrétiennes 76
(1961), 173–203. Introduction and
Latin text, French transl.

Lawson, Sr R. Penelope, *The Pastoral Prayer of St Aelred of
Rievaulx* (1955). English transl.

Sr Rose of Lima, "The Pastoral Prayer," in Hoste, A., ed.,
*For Criste Luve: Prayers of St Aelred of
Rievaulx* (1965), 39–54.
Latin/English; reprinted separately as *The
Pastoral Prayer* (1968).

Walsh, J., ed., "The Prayer of a Superior," *The Way* (July,
1964), 231–5.

References to translations into Dutch and German are in
Hoste, A., *Bibliotheca Aelrediana,* Instrumenta Patristica
II (1962), 83f, to which add a Latin/Spanish edition,
Gomez de las Barcenas, A. and Leym de Castro, L., *La
Oracion Pastoral de San Eldredo, Abad de Rieval,* Cistercium
12 (1960), 172–85.

This work was not generally known until Dom André
Wilmart discovered it in Jesus College, Cambridge in
1925: it is not in Migne.

II. GENERAL STUDIES OF ST AELRED AND HIS WRITINGS

Above all others must stand this work, resulting from a 1958 Oxford thesis:

Squire, A., *Aelred of Rievaulx: a Study* (1969).

a. Historical Aspect

    Knowles, M. D., *The Monastic Order in England* (1940), 239–66 passim. 2nd ed. 1963 makes no change. Reprinted in *Saints and Scholars* (1962), 34–50.

    Powicke, F. M., "Aelred of Rievaulx," *Ways of Medieval Life and Thought* (1949), 7–26.
        Walter Daniel's Life of Aelred, Abbot of Rievaulx (1950).

    Squire, A., "Historical Factors in the Formation of Aelred of Rievaulx," *Collectanea O.C.R.* 22 (1960), 263–83.
        "Aelred and King David," *ib.* 356–77.
        "Aelred and the Northern Saints," *ib.* 23 (1961), 58–69.

    Stacpoole, A. J., "The Public Face of Aelred," *Downside Review* 85 (1967), 183–99, 318–25.

b. Spiritual and Theological Aspect

    Brooke, O., "Towards a Theology of Connatural Knowledge," *Cîteaux* 18 (1967), 275–90.

    Burridge, A., "The Spirituality of St Aelred," *Downside Review* 58 (1940), 225–47.

    Dumont C., "St Aelred: the Balanced Life of a Monk," *Monastic Studies* 1 (1963), 25–38; transl. of art. in *Collectanea O.C.R.* 18 (1956), 177–89.

Hallier, A., *The Monastic Theology of Aelred of Rievaulx*, Cistercian Studies 2 (1969); transl. of *Un Éducateur Monastique, Aelred de Rievaulx* (1959).

Squire, A., "Aelred of Rievaulx and the Monastic Tradition concerning Action and Contemplation," *Downside Review* 72 (1954), 289–303.

III. STUDIES RELATING TO THE TREATISES

The introductions to the three treatises in Sources Chrétiennes 60 and 76 should be consulted. It will be noticed that the treatise *De Jesu Puero Duodenni*, which had a wide circulation in England and on the Continent during the Middle Ages, has not received the attention it deserves from modern scholars.

a. A Rule of Life for a Recluse

This has been widely (but not closely) studied by scholars: cf. *Bibliotheca Aelrediana*, 78–80 where twenty-two studies are listed.

Talbot, C. H., "Le Mysticisme du Traité *de Institutione Inclusarum* de Saint Elrède," *Collectanea O.C.R.* 6 (1940), 246–54.

b. The Pastoral Prayer

Courcelle, P., "Aelred de Rievaulx à l'Ecole des Confessions," *Revue des Etudes Augustiniennes* 3 (1957), 163–74.

Wilmart, A., *Auteurs Spirituels et Textes Dévots du Moyen Age Latin* (1932), 287–91.

ANALYTIC INDEX

Numbers refer to paragraphs in the texts. The following abbreviations are used: JT = *Jesus at the Age of Twelve*; PP = *The Pastoral Prayer*; RR = *A Rule of Life for a Recluse*.

Abbot, JT 30f; RR 7; PP 1ff
   see also Aelred of Rievaulx
Abel, JT 15
Abraham, JT 18
   bosom of, RR 33
Acedia (spiritual weariness), JT 30,
   34; RR 9
Action, relation to contemplation,
   JT 30f
Active life, RR 28
Adam, RR 11
Adultery, the woman taken in, RR 31
Aelred of Rievaulx, St, JT 1; RR 18,
   22, 32
   his parents, RR 32
   his sister, RR 1
   pastoral prayer, PP 1ff
   refrains from taking a position
     where there are different theo-
     logical opinions, JT 10
   sinfulness, RR 32; PP 2, 5
Affection, JT 11; RR 33
Agnes, St, RR 16
Alms giving, RR 3f, 28, 33
Andrew, St, Apostle, RR 31
Angels, JT 7f, 12, 21, 26; RR 11, 14,
   29, 31, 33
   guardian, RR 16
   paradise, RR 24
Anger, RR 31
Annunciation, RR 29
Apostles, JT 9, 16

   see also St Andrew, St James, St John
     the Evangelist, Judas, St Paul,
     St Peter
Archangels, JT 7
Avarice, RR 3, 31, 33

Baptism, RR 26
   of Christ, JT 7; RR 31
Beatitude, JT 10
Benedict, St, RR 12
Bethany, RR 31
Bethlehem, JT 3, 19
   house of bread, JT 3, 11
   signifies the beginning of a good
     life, JT 19
Birth, RR 32
   of Christ, RR 29
   spiritual, JT 12, 19
   see also Conversion
Blessed Sacrament, *see* Holy Eucharist
Boasting, RR 24
Body, to be sacrificed for the sake of
   the soul, RR 23

Cain, JT 15; RR 32
Canaanites, the unclean spirits, JT 14
Celibacy, RR 14
   see also Chastity, Virginity
Charity, JT 24; RR 16, 25ff, 33
   Christ's, RR 31
   fraternal, JT 30f
   mother, JT 30f